What You Don't Know About Know About Retirement Will Hurt You!

Dan McGrath & Michael Gerali

with

Justin Belair, Robert Klein, John Marroni,
Robert Ryerson, and Mike Padawer

Table of Contents

Prologue...5

Introduction...11

1   The 3 Rules of the New Retirement.....................................19

2   But Will This Affect Me?...43

3   And Your Costs Are …...49

4   How Are Medicare Part B Premiums Determined?.......57

5   How Are Medicare Part D Premiums Determined?.......59

6   What Happened to My Social Security Check?.................63

7   To Have and to Hold...75

8   Medical Expense Deduction..81

9   The Three Holy Grails of Health Care Planning............85

10   Hey Mom, Can We Talk?...91

11   Why Is My Financial Adviser Recommending an Annuity?.....105

12   What's The Deal with Long-Term Care?.........................123

13   The Changing Landscape of Estate Planning................131

14   The Facts About Reverse Mortgages.................................139

Afterword...147

About the Authors..153

Prologue
By Dan McGrath

When my mother turned 65 a few years ago, she found herself in the position of trying to decipher the rules of Social Security and Medicare. Like most retirees, she wanted simple answers and didn't bother to read the fine print too carefully. Besides, she had worked and saved and invested throughout her life, and she thought that she was well prepared for retirement.

At the time I was a Senior VP of Sales for a small money management firm. My job description was to travel the country and give investment information to financial advisors. The goal was to build deep relationships with these financial advisors by giving them advice on what were the best practices across the country and to see if the firm I represented was a fit. Ultimately, my job was to find out what was working for others and then let others know about it.

In the financial industry my real label was "wholesaler" and the tag line that goes with the title is *"the guy with no real-world experience when working with investors, but the guy who had the budget to market."*

I worked very hard to set myself apart from this label while also using my access to some of the best planners in the country, to learn all of the "ins and outs" of financial planning. I conducted elaborate seminars and client appreciation nights. I attended client meetings. All the while, I asked questions when I deemed them relevant. From this access I started to develop a simplistic overall financial plan that almost anyone could use.

In just a few short years, I learned how to build specific investment strategies for any type of investor and even developed a specific niche for retirees. Just by asking a person a few pertinent questions I could determine what was the proper asset allocation (how much invested in risky investments along with how much in "safe" investments) for them.

All I had to do was to choose which types of investments to put into the allocation. Analyzing specific mutual funds, separate accounts, bonds and even stocks became second nature for me. I would line up the Alpha, the Sharpe Ratio and the correlation of the indexes and voilà, I knew which investments worked with which goals and needs, and I could adjust the potential performance of the models to reflect the person's risk tolerance.

The models were simple, efficient, and cheap and even better, there was never a need for those pesky annuities or that even worse product, life insurance.

My mantra was "the market will take of everything" and I spread it to anyone and everyone who would listen.

I had done IT! I had built the perfect investing strategy for anyone who was either in or heading into retirement. I was, at least in my mind, brilliant. I could do anything!

Then a funny thing happened.

As I had said, my mother was turning 65 years old. She was worried about what to do next. She phoned me and asked me one simple question. And from there my fall from grace happened relatively quickly.

Mom: "I'm turning 65 and think I have to sign up for Medicare. What do I need to do?"

Me (mister smart guy): "Mom, I don't do that, I help people plan for retirement. Medicare is free and what is the big deal? Just call someone in the government and everything will be fine. Now, do you want to know how my great model is working for you today?"

Mom: "I guess."

Well, my mother contacted the Medicare office and explained her situation—or at least part of it. She didn't think to include a few things, such as my dad's pension and the health benefits she received through the pension. My mother enrolled in Medicare parts A, B, D and obtained a supplemental policy. Then, thinking she was fully covered, she let the pension coverage lapse.

Within the year of her turning 65, my mother needed to have some serious dental work done. Apparently, there was an infection in her gum line and there was a need to have some of her teeth extracted.

My sister, who's a registered nurse and I never gave it a second thought. Our mother was in pain and needed help. Get her to a dentist and get the procedure done as quickly as possible."

Once there, she got the shock of a lifetime: the cost.

A tooth extraction was roughly $3,000 per tooth, and my mother needed four teeth pulled. The cost would be over $12,000. And that didn't include tax.

My sister, surprisingly calm at this moment, simply said, "Mom, don't worry. You have insurance through Dad's pension from the jail. (My father was a Corrections Officer for 25 years before passing away two years after retirement at the old age of 52) This should be covered, right?"

The dentist chimed in: "Medicare doesn't cover dental work, so I am afraid the cost is the cost. If you do have another form of insurance, we could take that."[1]

Things went from bad to worse when my mother explained to us that when she signed up for Medicare, she thought that she was fully insured since she enrolled into Part A, B, and D, and even a supplemental policy, too. Because of this, she let the other insurance my father's pension supplied lapse.

My sister was livid. "Did you speak to anyone about the coverage or the options you had, Mom? Because of the pension and the benefits

[1] http://www.cms.gov/Medicare/Coverage/MedicareDentalCoverage/index.html?redirect=/MedicareDentalCoverage/

from Dad's job, you have the chance to have something that not everyone will have: the opportunity to be fully insured. Most people will never have that chance since all they will be able to enroll in is either Original Medicare or a Medicare Advantage Plan, and these plans never cover everything. In fact, Original Medicare will never cover routine dental work, vision, hearing, or even podiatry. And Medicare Advantage Plans will only cover these things if you pay through the teeth for them. But with Dad's health benefits from work, you had this all taken care of. What happened?"

Our mother replied, "I spoke to your brother, but he couldn't help me."

My sister, stunned and shocked, now turned all her anger and rage at me, and of course you could guess what she said. It was not even close to "Happy Birthday."

She asked one simple question: "Why?"

Me (defensively): "It's not what I do. I help people plan for retirement. I help them build financial plans that will last them through their retirement and longer."

My sister: "What do you think retirement is? Do you think its playing golf every day for the next 200 years? Do you think it's going out to eat for every meal or building a dream house or taking vacations every other week? What do you think retirement is?"

Me (hesitantly):" I'm not sure now. I guess it would plan for everything, including health care"

My sister: "Everything? That's rich! I guess it could be everything in the first five to ten years of retirement, but what do you think happens when people reach 80 or 85 and older? Do you think they are still going out to eat every day, going on vacation every day? It is people like you who are the problem. I see people every day stuck in a position of choosing their health over things like food or happiness. I see the quality of life deteriorating for people because they didn't enroll into Medicare properly or didn't plan appropriately. Yes, they got the money thing half right, I suppose, but didn't you ever stop to think about what else there is? These people who you talk to are expecting you to advise them, for you to help them. They depend on you, and in the end what do you really know?"

I was floored. Not only had I let my own mother down, my sister utterly destroyed any sense of well-being I had concerning my job or self-importance. I quickly realized that I knew absolutely nothing when it came to retirement. And for all of the self-congratulating I gave myself, it didn't matter one bit.

Yes, I could build financial plans for people based on their risk tolerance or their goals. Yes, I could create investment models that in turn would help them financially over the long term. But what did that matter if it was for the wrong purpose, or if it left them with huge exposures on the health care front?

If the people I thought I was helping didn't know what their goals were because they didn't know what the problems may be, then how could I build anything correctly?

And, unfortunately, I would come to realize that I was wrong about the investments, too. Once I dove into this topic, I found out quickly that I was dead wrong.

I also realized that if even a seasoned investment professional like me was unaware of issues in retirement that could hurt everyone, how could the average person navigate through their retirement without hitting the rocks occasionally?

I began the idea for this book by speaking with people I knew and trusted, in order to understand the truths, and the misconceptions about the "new retirement". I was determined to learn from the experience with my mom and ensure that people became aware of the things about retirement that so many of them were totally unaware of.

As you will be able to see when reading this book, investing in the stock market or in bonds, or any investments, is all just part of an overall plan. There are many other aspects that need to be integrated with the investment piece; without them, those investments may wind up being of limited value, no matter how steadily they may rise.

Because as I've learned, the things that we don't know about retirement will hurt not only us, but our families as well!

We would like to thank our families.

Without their help and understanding, this book would never have gotten off the ground.

Josh Jackson for his hard work and dedication.

Hans Schemmel for his direction.

Carl Robinson for always believing in the concept.

Chris Leone for his painstaking time and effort making sure that we were always on track.

Warren Watson for his guidance over the last 25 years.

Kurt Fasen for his support on this project.

Kevin McGarry for his vision and commitment to discussing health care costs.

And especially Bob Peatman of Weston Capital Partners, whose foresight was the reason why this information was even researched in the first place.

Introduction
By Michael Gerali

From doctors to teachers to financial advisors to the clergy—we have always turned to those with the greatest levels of skills, experience, knowledge, and capabilities to help guide us through life, in the healthiest, wealthiest, most knowledgeable, and morally right manner. Since few of us are well versed in all these areas, we turn to these "experts" to lead us on a path that is the most fulfilling for our lives, whether that is for 100 years or a lot shorter period of time.

On a regular basis, however, and all around us, we are struck by the inaccuracies in the information that some of these leaders provide to us, which can cause us to question the guidance we have received, even when there appears to be confirmation or agreement from other sources. Whether it is scandals marring the church's record, or research revealing that the accepted food pyramid might lead to diabetes, we are awakening to the fact that what we've learned is often, in fact, incorrect.

The book you are about to read will highlight another of these awakening experiences. It is not designed to point fingers, cast judgment, or illustrate the incompetency of any one industry. It was written by a group of individuals concerned about the future retirements of the largest population segment in the United States, and its lack of awareness regarding one of the largest expenses it will incur.

This book is designed to be a wake-up call for its readers to better understand that what they have been taught about planning for retirement by their parents, financial advisors, and the media has missed a key expense component which will eclipse all others at some point in the course of retirement: health care costs.

This book was written by seven financial planning professionals with over a century of combined experience in the industry, who are nervously watching future health care costs grow exponentially for retirees *without* seeing any shifts in their financial planning for retirement. As Dan McGrath, one of the co-authors of this book states, "I feel like I am standing on the bow of the Titanic screaming and pointing at an iceberg and no one in the bridge is willing to turn the wheel to avoid it!"

Much of the information in this book has been derived from the Affordable Care Act, Medicare and Medicaid, and other readily available sources provided by the government regarding population trends and retirement mechanics . None of this information would cost you money to obtain, nor would you have to order it for delivery. Any search engine would take you to this information. The question is, who is willing to read it and put it all together neatly? For example, the original 2,700 page Affordable Care Act was so large and so quickly pushed through Congress that no one really had a chance to read, digest, and understand the implications of it prior to voting on the bill. In addition, Medicare and Medicaid are changing so quickly each year that trying to stay on top of them requires the same commitment that a CPA has to staying on top of tax law changes.

At the heart of the issue is the fact that we are moving toward a perfect storm of population imbalance, increasing longevity, higher-than average inflation of costs relating to medicine and eldercare, and a population of uninformed current and future retirees. Unfortunately the Baby Boomer generation has modeled their retirement planning and expectations on those of the "Greatest Generation". With significantly longer life expectancies, however, and over 10,000 Baby Boomers turning 65 every day for the next 17 years[2], there will be a greater need for more comprehensive health care to handle the elderly. This will be coupled with a smaller financial population behind them, to support them! Greater

2 http://www.pewsocialtrends.org/2010/12/20/baby-boomers-approach-65-glumly/

costs, plus fewer people to cover the bill for government entitlements, will realistically result in higher premiums paid by those utilizing the benefits. It really is simple mathematics!

Let's look at current retirees for a moment. On average, health care costs account for 33% of their overall expenditures[3]. These can be costs as fixed as long-term care annual premiums, annual doctor visits, or a new pair of glasses every couple of years, or as variable as hospital-stay deductibles, changes to coverage of drug copays, or short-term disability costs tied to a significant surgery or injury.

Most financial planners have accounted for these costs to a certain extent as a part of their general financial plans for clients. They project estimates of annual fixed costs and include a "rainy day fund" for unexpected additional expenditures. If you talk with the average financial advisor, most will tell you that they understand that out-of-pocket medical costs will go up as retirees get older, but that those costs may be offset by less spending on golf, travel, etc., and that these savings may cover the additional health care costs. When confronted with the question of "how much more" it may be for an 80-year old's out-of-pocket costs compared to those of a 65-year old, they will often quote the overall averages, and that is what they use as a part of the financial plan.

Averages! As we all know, we are not average. We are all different! It is fine to apply averages to set expectations, but at the end of the day, some people are going to pay more for out-of-pocket costs while some are going to pay less. However, since we do not know who is who on this front, we need to plan for the worst.

The irony is that many of the people we think are going to face the highest costs in terms of out-of-pocket expenses, will generally face the least! By the same token, we always talk about how the healthier a person is going into retirement, the less they will end up spending for health care costs. We have been taught that if you eat healthful foods, exercise regularly, don't drink or smoke or do drugs, you will live a long life and not run into health issues.

3 http://bipartisanpolicy.org/sites/default/files/BPC%20Health%20Care%20Cost%20 Drivers%20Brief%20Sept%202012.pdf

Yes, this is generally correct, but this is also why those people in the best shape will ultimately have to pay more out-of-pocket for their costs. Those in the best of health are going to live the longest![4]

The person with diabetes, heart disease, high blood pressure, cancer, and other factors of "unhealthiness" will ultimately generally face significantly lower out-of-pocket medical costs because they will die earlier! The over-weight 69-year-old golfer who keels over of a heart-attack on the 7th hole will generate significantly less costs than the non-red meat eating distance runner who lives to 90 years old but who faces the potential for cancer, Alzheimer's, and kidney failure.

In the Bay Area, there is a financial advisor who competes in triathlons who built his entire practice by first selling long-term care insurance to other triathletes who believed that their healthy lifestyle would absolve their need for such insurance. After a 10 minute talk to this advisor about the cold hard facts—that their quality of life could actually increase their potential for long-term care needs (compounded by the potential for injuries or hip and knee replacements), most of his clients turn to him for their full financial planning.

So we now have a population of retirees and pre-retirees, who have been conditioned to eat healthful foods, reduce stress, exercise, sleep well, and generally do everything possible to be able to extend their lifespan. This is great on the individual level, but as we start to take a long hard look at the implications on a national scale, the figures start to become astronomical.

Social Security has been in the spotlight for the last decade or so with most of the news revolving around the question of whether it will still be in place in 20 years because of the baby boomer generation. Why?

When Social Security was first implemented, it was designed to assist those who were outliving the "average" life expectancy and it was a way to add an additional stream of income for those individuals. When Social Security was implemented in 1935[5], the average life expectancy was

4 http://www.huffingtonpost.com/2013/07/29/life-expectancy_n_3670934.html
5 http://www.ssa.gov/history/hfaq.html

58 for men and 62 for women[6] and the benefit kicked in at age 65. Now, the average life expectancy is 78.7 years[7]. So instead of it supplementing income for those who <u>lived well past the average</u>, and with the average life expectancy being significantly longer than age 65, more than 50% of retirees are living many years under the umbrella of Social Security.

Now, apply this same concept to Medicare. The same population of retirees who are taking Social Security will be enrolling in Medicare as well (it is actually required to receive your Social Security). Keep three factors in mind on this front: the baby boomers will live significantly longer in retirement than the "Greatest Generation," the inflationary increases in costs for health care is generally double to triple that of goods and services; and the population of the next generation of earners who will be supporting the baby boomers in retirement will be significantly smaller that the population of baby boomers.[8]

So, who is going to pay for Medicare? Those who are using it, of course! Based on the above information, it should be common sense for people to expect their Medicare premiums to go up. But by how much? And what are the factors that determine how much one person pays versus another? This is where the critical financial planning component for retirement income comes into play.

However, what the current and future Medicare participant fails to understand is that virtually all assets are available to be included in the calculation for the annual premiums. This includes their house (when sold), retirement accounts, Social Security, pensions, estate settlements, and all other avenues of income (whether they are taxable or not). With few exceptions, Medicare will take into account ALL income available to determine what the participant will pay in premiums.

Yes, there are a few exceptions. Is your financial planner talking with you about what these exceptions are? Our guess is no. Is the media? Definitely not! As a part of the solutions aspect of this book, we will outline <u>important matters</u> about retirement, such as how investors can utilize

6 http://www.ssa.gov/history/lifeexpect.html
7 http://www.cdc.gov/nchs/fastats/lifexpec.htm
8 http://www.ssa.gov/policy/docs/ssb/v66n4/v66n4p37.html

these few exceptions to protect themselves from significantly higher premiums based on the current Medicare laws.

For example, let's take a quick quiz: Where is the number one place we have been told to invest no matter how much or little cash you have to spare? Answer: The employer match 401(k) plan.

Why is this supposedly such a great idea? The assumption is that this will allow your money to grow tax-deferred for a long time, and that when you start taking out income from these accounts in retirement, your tax rate will be lower than it was during your "working" years. Today, with more and more companies moving away from traditional pensions in favor of defined contribution plans, 401(k)s are now an integral part of most employees' benefits packages, and there is an enormous amount of money tied up in these tax deferred accounts.

So what is the downside? When retirees are taking income from these plans (or at least the Required Minimum Distributions as required by the IRS), the distributions from these vehicles are considered income in the eyes of Medicare, as well as the IRS and states. The more income that is taken from these tax-deferred savings vehicles, the more income that is included in the means testing formula which determines your Medicare premiums.

Here's another quick quiz: Is your current financial advisor incorporating this factor into your plan? Is he or she working with you to offer alternatives to your investments in order to avoid having your income increasing your premiums? Does he or she even know about this factor? Are they recommending moving money from IRA accounts to other vehicles to protect you from the long term effects of these calculations?

Again, we are not focused on pointing fingers; however, what you don't know about retirement will hurt you, and even your financial planner may be unaware of these facts! At the time of the printing of this book, for example, this information was not included in the Certified Financial Planner (CFP) educational materials.

Why is this important? Because the cost of your premiums is going to be one of the largest expenses that you will pay as a retiree. And, as more and more people turn 65 and participate in Medicare, the more these costs are going to increase.

The goal of this book is to open your eyes to some of the largest expenses that you will incur in retirement. It is an effort to illustrate what is currently going on with the Affordable Care Act, Medicare, and Medicaid, to assist you in being better prepared for these inevitable costs.

The authors of this book have gotten together to give you direction as an investor (and/or to assist your financial advisor) in putting together a financial plan that meets your retirement income needs AND protects you from such things as inflated Medicare premiums and surcharges in retirement.

Is it time that we amend the old saying to be that "the only guarantees in life are death, taxes, and rising health care costs"? With a disproportionate percentage of the US population turning 65 over a 20-year period and living significantly longer in retirement, the one thing that we're certain of is that the costs for health care are going to increase.

This book will lay out this information in detail and provide insights into how you can address what you, and many "financial professionals" don't yet know about retirement.

The question is: What are you going to do with this information?

The 3 Rules of the New Retirement
By Dan McGrath

Rule 1: Medicare, your gift from the government.

Did you know that you had a mandatory expense in retirement?

As I sat at the table with my mother, I calmly explained what I had learned throughout my research on this subject of health costs, retirement and financial planning.

I informed her that long before the Affordable Care Act, better known as Obamacare, rolled around, believe or not, there was already a mandate in place that stated you needed to have health insurance or else. This law was not something new, as it was something that retirees have had to deal with for years.

Once you are 65 years or older, have retired from work, or are no longer covered by an employer's or spouse's employer's health insurance plan, and are collecting Social Security, you <u>must</u> accept Medicare Part A.

My mother quickly stated, "But Medicare Part A is free, so what is the big deal?"

On the surface it may not seem like a big deal, as she was correct that Part A is technically free since it is the coverage that most people who pay into Social Security will also pay for while they are employed, but there are other Parts of Medicare as well, and they are not free.

Once you accept Part A and are no longer covered by creditable health insurance you must enroll into Medicare Parts B & D or face late enrollment penalties[9] that last for the rest of your life.

"What???" my mother asked.

I explained to her that, yes, she heard me correct and I apologized for not knowing this when she turned 65, but I was hoping to redeem myself now.

The late enrollment penalty I explained is for anyone who decides to delay enrollment into Medicare Parts B & D past their Initial Enrollment Period (IEP)[10], which is either their 65th birthday or the 8 months after they officially are no longer covered by creditable health insurance.

The penalties are as follows:

For Part B[11]: For each 12 month period that you delay enrolling into Medicare part B you will receive a 10% penalty on top of your premium. So if you delay 36 months and the Part B premium is say $125 a month you will pay that $125 a month plus a 30% charge on top of that each month too. If that premium increases in the next subsequent years then that 30% surcharge will also follow those new costs too, you will ultimately pay that extra 30% for the rest of your life.

For Part D[12]: For each month delayed you will be charged 1%, and this percent will also follow you for the rest of your life. So if you go those 3 years without enrolling, Medicare will charge you 1% for each month missed or 36% more on top of the National Base Premium, which in 2013 is $31.17

"So there are late enrollment penalties too, anything else?" she asked

Just one little thing, those people who do retire, who are now no longer covered by creditable health insurance and are 65 or older must

9 http://www.medicare.gov/your-medicare-costs/part-b-costs/penalty/part-b-late-enrollment-penalty.html

10 http://www.medicare.gov/Pubs/pdf/11219.pdf

11 http://www.medicare.gov/your-medicare-costs/part-b-costs/penalty/part-b-late-enrollment-penalty.html

12 http://www.medicare.gov/part-d/costs/penalty/part-d-late-enrollment-penalty.html

accept Medicare or face also the possibility of forfeiting their Social Security benefit[13].

"Forfeit Social Security benefits, what is this? "My mother screamed.

"Well, err…" I stuttered as I responded to her and quickly tried to eyeball the room to see if there was a huge wooden spoon in the vicinity.

During my childhood, my mother, a hot tempered Sicilian woman from the East side of Boston, ruled the house with two very unique tools: a large wooden spoon and for when times called for harsher measures, a large wooden fork.

To this day when I see either of those utensils displayed in someone's house or even at a store, I quickly cringe and look down at my knuckles as I remember the pain.

Unfortunately, as I stated to my mom, if someone is collecting Social Security, they must also accept Medicare when eligible, and if they do not enroll into Medicare for some reason at that time, then yes, they forfeit their Social Security benefits.

"What about those people who started collecting Social Security at age 62?" she asked.

"Even those people who opted to collect Social Security benefits at age 62 have to enroll once eligible or they will have to pay back every cent they ever collected…every cent."

My mother was dumbfounded at this news. She couldn't believe that people really didn't have a choice when it came to health costs in retirement and that the punishment they faced was both a late penalty that lasted for their rest of their life and quite possibly the forfeiture of any Social Security benefit they may be entitled to.

"Why hasn't anyone ever told me about this? Why isn't anyone doing anything about this? Isn't there anyone helping people plan for this?

13 http://www.elderlawanswers.com/you-can39t-opt-out-of-medicare-without-losing-social-security-judge-rules-9017

Anyone? "She was almost pleading, and what was strange was that I was sort of happy on the inside that she wasn't angry since I knew that any anger she had would still likely be directed at me.

As for anyone doing anything about this, well there was a landmark court case that was settled back in 2012, docket No. 11-5076, Hall vs. Sibelius[14].

On October 9, 2008, Brian Hall, a retired employee of the Department of Housing and Urban Development; Lewis Randall, a member of the board of directors of E*Trade; and Norman Rogers, retired founder and CEO of Rabbit Semiconductor, filed a lawsuit alleging that the 1993 and 2002 rules added by the Social Security Administration to its "Program Operations Manual" were illegal.[15] Their complaint centered around the provision that any retiree who elects to opt out of Medicare Part A will automatically lose Social Security retirement benefits and will be forced to repay any Social Security benefits received prior to opting out of Medicare Part A.

The plaintiffs' argument went like this:

- Both the Social Security Act and Medicare Act state clearly that applying for the programs is voluntary and that an application for one of the programs is not dependent on application for the other. So the new SSA rules to make enrolling in Medicare mandatory violates the Social Security Act and Medicare Act as well as Article I, Section 1 of the Constitution.

- Forced participation in Medicare infringes on a citizen's right to privacy and violates that individual's right to make necessary choices about his or her own health care, and, accordingly, violates the First, Fourth, Fifth, Ninth, and Fourteenth Amendments to the Constitution.

- The new SSA rules were put into place without undergoing the "notice" and "comment" rule-making requirements. The policies should have been published in the Federal Register and made open to com-

---

14 http://www.cadc.uscourts.gov/internet/opinions.
nsf/890596479218E0818525799D00548389/$file/11-5076-1356903.pdf
15 http://www.thefundforpersonalliberty.org/medicare-lawsuit-update/

ment by the general public prior to implementation. Not doing this violated the Federal Administrative Procedure Act.

Federal Judge Rosemary M. Collyer dismissed the case on March 16, 2011, saying that "requiring a mechanism for Plaintiffs and others in their situation to 'dis-enroll' would be contrary to Congressional intent, which was to provide 'mandatory' benefits under Medicare Part A for those receiving Social Security Retirement benefits."[16]

The ruling was based on a principle called "Congressional intent." In other words, it was based on the conclusion that "An individual is statutorily entitled to Medicare Part A upon becoming entitled to monthly Social Security retirement benefits (SSRB). Thus, anyone who 'is entitled' to SSRB 'shall be entitled' to Medicare Part A benefits immediately upon his 65th birthday."[17]

The ruling went on to state that "Under the Social Security Act: Every individual who (1) is fully insured, has attained age 62, and has filed an application for old-age insurance benefits (Social Security benefits) shall be entitled to old-age insurance benefit[s] as well. To be 'entitled' to SSRB, then, an individual must also "apply" as well; if he fails to file an application, he is not 'entitled' to the benefits regardless of his age or working history."[18]

An appellate court upheld Judge Collyer's ruling, on January 11, 2013 and unfortunately the U.S. Supreme Court declined to hear the case.

So the answer to my mother's plea of someone doing something about this was and is yes, but the problem is that the results of their efforts were negative. This rule stands: In order to collect Social Security benefits you must accept Medicare when eligible. This now means that you have a new certainty in retirement:

Along with the other two certainties in life, death and taxes, there are now also health care costs, and as my mother asked, who is helping you plan for this?

16 http://www.benefitspro.com/2011/05/10/bail-on-medicare-part-a-and-youll-lose-social-secu
17 Court Case Hall vs. Sibelius No. 11-5076
18 Court Case Hall vs. Sibelius No. 11-5076

Think about it. People create financial plans and budgets all the time. They build them on the internet in their free time as retirement creeps closer and closer, or for those who have a financial advisor, there is usually a discussion on future plans at almost every meeting. But when has anyone, any calculator, or any company ever asked you about your future health costs?

Yes, investment firms and financial professionals will help you fill buckets with money which are ear marked for certain expenses like a house or mortgage, or travel and vacations, but some simpler questions needs to be asked:

Does the government state that you have to have a mortgage?

Does the government state that you must own a car or buy food?

Or even, does the government take away your Social Security benefit if you decide to not take a vacation?

The answer today, which may change in a few years, is a resounding no to all three of those questions, but the problem that we all now face is that the government is saying this exactly about health costs:

It is stating that you have to incur health costs (in the form of premiums for Medicare), and if you don't accept them, you won't collect Social Security. What's even worse is that when you do finally enroll into this expense, if it is too late, you will be faced with ridiculously high late penalties that will remain with you for the rest of your life!

Conclusion to the first rule; *Medicare is Mandatory*:

Today, as millions of Americans prepare to retire, many are woefully underestimating the true cost of their future health insurance and health care. And like it or not, both health insurance and health care are now mandatory expenses for all of us.

Because of the law, we all must realize the following:

- You have to enroll into Medicare when you become eligible or you will forfeit Social Security.[19]

- If you start receiving Social Security benefits at age 62, but do not enroll into Medicare when you become eligible at age 65, you will have to pay back every penny you have received from Social Security.[20]

- This law was created in 1993 and has been upheld by the Courts as recently as 1/11/2013.[21]

- As of right now, Medicare Part B premiums, along with any late fees, are automatically deducted from any Social Security benefit you may receive.[22]

- If your Social Security benefit is not large enough to cover the costs of the premiums and the penalties, you will be sent a bill for the difference.[23]

- Medicare is inflating at roughly 7% or higher, and Social Security's cost-of-living adjustments are expected to be only 2.8% at a maximum for the foreseeable future.[24]

- When planning for the cost of living out in your golden years, you need to figure in the true cost of health insurance and health care because they are the only mandatory costs you will have.[25]

My question to you:
Is your advisor or financial firm helping you to plan for this?

---

19 http://www.elderlawanswers.com/you-can39t-opt-out-of-medicare-without-losing-social-security-judge-rules-9017
20 http://www.elderlawanswers.com/you-can39t-opt-out-of-medicare-without-losing-social-security-judge-rules-9017
21 Congressional Research Service for Congress–Medicare: Part B Premiums June 2013
22 Congressional Research Service for Congress–Medicare: Part B Premiums June 2013
23 http://www.network13.org/FRM/Section_11/11E_SSA_Premium_Info.pdf
24 http://www.ssa.gov/OACT/TR/TRassum.html
25 The Patient Protection and Affordable Care Act

Rule 2: You have to be kidding—the more you make the more you pay?!

My mother after hearing this was no longer confused, or even pleading. She was downright fit to be tied.

"YOU MEAN MEDICARE IS GOING TO LOOK AT HOW MUCH INCOME I HAVE, THEN DECIDE ON WHAT I AM GOING TO PAY?"

The answer, which I tried to rephrase in a more delicate way, was basically, Yup.

Medicare is means tested or more to the point: Medicare uses your income to determine what you will you be paying for part B & D premiums, and to make matters worse, if you are subject to this means testing, Medicare will automatically deduct any surcharges directly from your Social Security benefit as well as your Part B premium (currently, there is still an option of how to fund Part D premiums. People can choose to have Social Security pay it directly or they can cover it themselves, but keep in mind that the surcharge will be coming out of any Social Security benefit).

As Michael Gerali, one of the lead contributors to this book likes to say to his clients or to anyone who will listen, "Funny, isn't it, that your income in retirement is really based on your income in retirement?".

What Mr. Gerali is alluding to is the fact that what you receive as Social Security income will have Medicare premiums and any surcharges automatically deducted from it and the amount of these deductions will be based squarely on your income.

So, your income in retirement is really based on your income in retirement. If you have too much, according to Medicare, then a portion of your income, Social Security, will be lowered through the guise of surcharges.

Well, my mother didn't find it the least bit funny, and the bigger problem that I now had on my hands was the simple fact that she had found that wooden spoon, and while staring at me the knuckles on her right hand had turned pure white.

I quickly sputtered that I was just the messenger and that I didn't do this, it wasn't me. Yes, I should have known this, as I put myself out there as a financial professional, but I rationalized that what I really did was a money thing, really just a money thing.

What I did, just like countless other financial professionals in the country, was create a plan for people to help them fund their retirement according to their "needs".

I babbled on about Sharpe Ratios, Alpha and Beta. I mentioned diversification, correlation and finally income, but my mother wasn't having any of it. "Messenger, you were supposed to know about this. People pay good money for your kind to help them and now you are telling me that what you did for me and for others is most likely going to be used against us later on?"

As a kid, that wooden spoon really did hurt, somehow she knew exactly where to hit. Whether it was on the knuckles or the fleshy part of the back of the arm or even the thigh—no matter where she got me it always hurt, and now as an adult I was worried it would be no different.

She may have lost some velocity with age, but it seemed like my flabbiness multiplied as I aged and no matter where she hit me it wouldn't matter and it would hurt like hell.

When she finally calmed down after what I counted from the red marks on hand and arms to be about a good 11 whacks, she wanted to know how this had happened and what it meant for her now.

I explained that back in 2003 Congress, along with the President, realized that seniors (instantly regretting using the term "seniors"), I mean retirees, were paying an exorbitantly large amount of money on prescription drugs, and there was no alternative for prescription coverage that could complement the health insurance coverage from Medicare, so they passed the Medicare Modernization Act, which created Medicare Advantage Plans and Prescription Drug Plans, or the "Part D" of Medicare.[26] Unfortunately, in the bill they passed, there was also language that

---

26 http://hpm.org/en/Surveys/Johns_Hopkins_Bloomberg_School_of__Publ._H_-_USA/09/
Means-testing_in_Medicare.html

called for those who would be deemed affluent retirees to pay a little more for their coverage since apparently they could afford it.

By 2007, Medicare had designed the first income brackets that they would implement relating to Part B and D premiums, along with penalties and amounts of how much each person who earned "too much income" would pay. Today the brackets that are used are as follows:

For Part B

If your yearly income in 2011 was		You pay (in 2013)
File individual tax return	File joint tax return	
$85,000 or less	$170,000 or less	$104.90 (25%)
Above $85,000 up to $107,000	Above $170,000 up to $214,000	$146.90 (35%)
Above $107,000 up to $160,000	Above $214,000 up to $320,000	$209.80 (50%)
Above $160,000 up to $214,000	Above $320,000 up to $428,000	$272.70 (65%)
Above $214,000	Above $428,000	$335.70 (80%)

For Part D

If your yearly income in 2011 was		You pay (in 2013)
File individual tax return	File joint tax return	
$85,000 or less	$170,000 or less	Your plan premium
Above $85,000 up to $107,000	Above $170,000 up to $214,000	Your plan premium + $11.60
Above $107,000 up to $160,000	Above $214,000 up to $320,000	Your plan premium + $29.90
Above $160,000 up to $214,000	Above $320,000 up to $428,000	Your plan premium + $48.10
Above $214,000	Above $428,000	Your plan premium + $66.40

Please keep in mind that under the proposed 2014 United States Presidential Budget (pages 38 & 39), there is a call to adjust these brackets until "25% of all beneficiaries will be subject to this cost." One of the proposals, from the Bipartisan Policy Center (BPC), a Congressional nonpartisan group, is calling for the following:[27]

For individuals earning	For couples	Part B (2017)	Part D (2017) Subject to change
$60k <	$90k <	No Penalty	No Penalty
$60k—$82k	$90k—$123k	Premium + 35%	Premium + $11.60
$82k—$135k	$123k—$202.5k	Premium + 50%	Premium + $29.90
$135k—$189k	$202.5k—$283k	Premium + 65%	Premium + $48.30
$189k +	$283k +	Premium + 80%	Premium + $66.60

Please note that there are no changes to the penalties, but that the income brackets are decreased by as little as 11% and as much as 47%, depending on your own personal situation.

Another proposal comes from the Ways and Means Committee[28]:

Beginning in 2017, this proposal would restructure income-related premiums under Medicare Parts B and D by increasing the lowest income-related premium five percentage points, from 35 percent to 40 percent, and also increasing premiums at higher income levels until capping the highest tier at 90 percent.

---

27 A Bipartisan Rx for Patient-Centered Care and System-Wide Cost Containment: Bi-Partisan policy Center April 2013

28 http://waysandmeans.house.gov/uploadedfiles/modernizing_cost-sharing_summary.pdf

For calendar years prior to 2017, if the modified adjusted gross income (single beneficiary) is:	For calendar years prior to 2017, the applicable percentage is:	For calendar years 2017 and later, if the modified adjusted gross income (single beneficiary) is:	For calendar years 2017 and later, the applicable percentage is:
More than $85,000 but not more than $107,000	35 percent	More than $85,000 but not more than $92,333	40.0 % of total premium
		More than $92,333 but not more than $99,667	46.5 % of total premium
		More than $99,667 but not more than $107,000	53.0 % of total premium
More than $107,000 but not more than $160,000	50 percent	More than $107,000 but not more than $124,667	59.5 % of total premium
		More than $124,667 but not more than $142,333	66.0 % of total premium
		More than $142,333 but not more than $160,000	72.5 % of total premium

More than $160,000 but not more than $214,000	65 percent	More than $160,000 but not more than $178,000	79.0 % of total premium
		More than $178,000 but not more than $196,000	85.5 % of total premium
		More than $196,000	90.0 % of total premium
More than $214,000	80 percent.		

This proposal is not calling for a lower bracket, but what it does call for is a slight increase in the percent of surcharges and for tweaks in a system already in place which may just ensnare a lot more retirees.

"You mean our government set this up and is looking for ways to make it worse?" My mom was shocked by this but I was elated that I could now play to the government being the bad people behind this and perhaps get away from that spoon.

One way to look at this, from a pure demographic viewpoint, is that there are plenty of Baby Boomers (roughly 76 to 78 million of them), and that for the last 40 to 60 years they have been not only changing the face of the world, but have been funding the government with revenue, or more to the point—tax dollars.

But now, where are they all headed?

Yes, retirement. The Baby Boomers are leaving the workforce and are heading for the easier side of life, and with them will go their tax dollars that the government has been using to fund itself.

This wouldn't be a problem if there were just as many people behind them in the next generation, those Gen Xers, but unfortunately there aren't.

According to the Bureau of Labor Statistics, depending on where you peg the Gen Xers (generally the 1965—1981 range) there are roughly anywhere from 50 to 62 million people in this cohort, which is far fewer than the baby boomer tsunami that blazed the path before them.

As you can see from this chart from the Bureau of Labor Statistics:

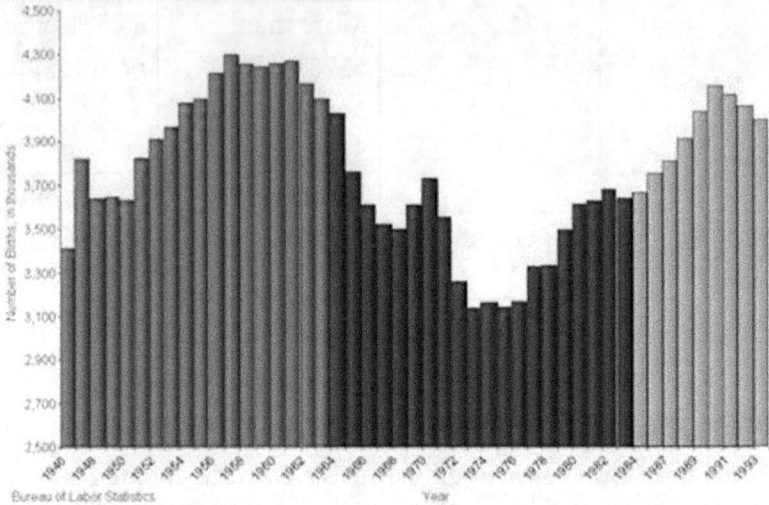

Bureau of Labor Statistics   Year

There is a significant drop off in people from Red, which represents the Baby Boomers, to the Blue, which represents Generation X, and the government is well aware of this.

The feds also have realized that the Baby Boomers have had 4 historic firsts in this country, and quite possibly the world:

1. They have earned the most amount of money ever (it's just pure size of the group plus inflation).

2. They have clearly spent more money than any one group before its time (even money they didn't have!).

3. They have hopefully saved the most amount of money any group has ever saved.

4. They have funded the government with the most amount of revenue it has ever had.

And again, where are they headed? Retirement.

Who is going to buy all the "stuff"? Who is going to earn the income? Who is going to take care of them as they age? Who is going to fund the government with needed tax revenues?

Well, if you dig deeper, it may just still be those Baby Boomers.

Back in 2007 the Congressional Budget Office released a chart on how Medicare, Social Security, and the overall Budget would look going forward in the future through 2080. It just happened to be released the same year that Medicare was going to be "means tested." Can you see anything odd?

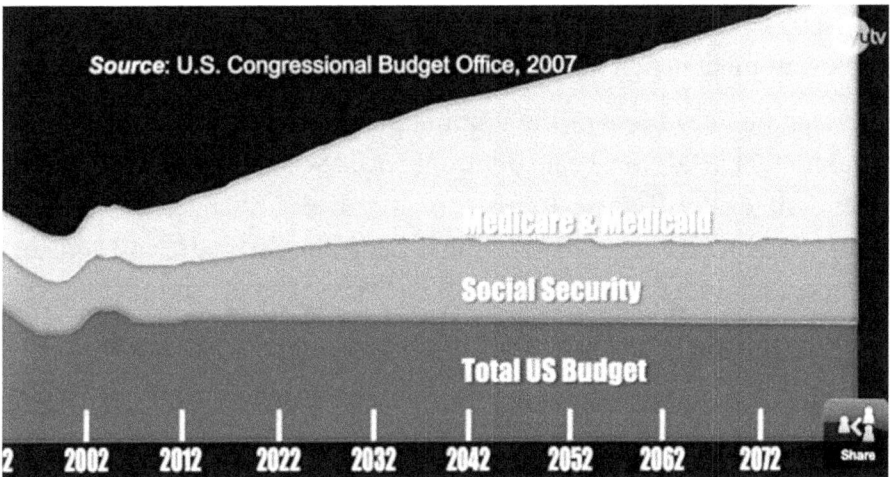

Source: U.S. Congressional Budget Office, 2007

Medicare & Medicaid

Social Security

Total US Budget

2002 2012 2022 2032 2042 2052 2062 2072

Medicare and Medicaid open up like a funnel in the mid 2020's, when the Boomers finally all retire, but for some reason Social Security and the Budget flat line. Could this be the fact that Medicare is means tested and that premiums, along with surcharges, will automatically be deducted from any Social Security benefits?

It may really be that simple. Medicare part B premiums, for the past 47 years, have been inflating at over 7.5% per year, but the projected cost of living adjustments(COLA's) for Social Security benefits are not expected to increase by more than 2.8% for the foreseeable future, according to the Social Security Board of Trustees 2012 report, under their "intermediate" assumptions section.

It would only be a matter of time before Medicare premiums would consume a large portion, if not a majority, of a person's Social Security benefit at these rates and these surcharges, for that "25% of all beneficiaries "that the government may target (as indicated in the proposed 2014 budget). This could explain why the projected budget remains constant in the 2007 GAO report .

My mom was floored, with the look of someone trying to put a puzzle together and just coming upon that one key piece. She stated, "It makes sense. Everyone knows that affording Social Security payments for the Baby Boomers will be difficult, but who has the brass stones to stand up in Congress and say anything? Whoever does will be tossed out almost immediately."

That one key piece of the funding puzzle is that they can lower the amount that needs to be paid out from Social Security by using Medicare premiums as the disguise. It's brilliant, it really is brilliant...very evil and very sad that it has come down to this, but from the politicians' and government's point of view, brilliant.

Conclusion to the second rule; *The more you make the more you pay!*

- Medicare is means tested, meaning it determines your Part B premiums solely on your income, while Part D is also impacted as well.

- The penalties currently range from 40% to 220% more.

- These penalties, and the associated income brackets, are currently being debated in Congress. There are proposals to have the income levels for surcharges lowered significantly, but for the penalties to remain the same.

- Even in the 2014 proposed Presidential Budget, on pages 38 and 39, there is language calling for not only this decrease in surcharge producing income brackets, but also for an increase in penalties, as well as a new 15% surcharge on any low cost sharing Medigap Plans as well.

Again, my question: Is your advisor or anyone in the financial industry helping you plan for this?

Rule 3:Your "income" is almost everything you can think of.

"WHAT????!!!!"What do you mean my income is almost everything?" My mom was back to having her blood boiling again.

I explained to her that the 3rd and final rule change for retirees is the simple fact that the income Medicare uses in its calculations is practically everything she had access to. This did not go over well.

Due to the legislative changes back in 2003 from the Medicare Modernization Act, income is now defined by Social Security as "the total of your adjusted gross income and any tax-exempt interest income you may have." These are the amounts on lines 37 and 8b of IRS form 1040".[29]

Some examples of what is defined as income are:

- Wages
- Social Security benefits
- Tips
- Pension income
- Rental income
- Capital gains (even the sale of your home will come into play)
- Dividends, including those from municipalities (The strategy your financial guy used to beat that new 3.8% Medicare tax on high income earners, by placing assets in municipal bonds doesn't work in retirement.)
- Withdrawals from certain annuities—(you need to find out what the "exclusion ratio" is for your annuity, if any. This would be the amount of income you receive that is not reported as taxable by the IRS).
- Withdrawals from 401(k)s
- Withdrawals from 403(b)s
- Withdrawals from 457 plans
- Withdrawals from SEP IRAs
- Withdrawals from Traditional IRA's

29 http://ssa-custhelp.ssa.gov/app/answers/detail/a_id/1601/~/calculation-of-modified-adjusted-gross-income-%28magi%29

Basically, the traditional financial plan for income in retirement is now going to be used against people when they retire.

As stated previously, Michael Gerali, a contributor to this book, has coined the adage, "Your income in retirement is based on your income in retirement."

Because of this 3rd rule, with your income including practically everything, the amount of net Social Security you will receive will come down to how much income you are earning. The more income from investments that you have, the higher the chance of your entering into another Medicare income bracket, thereby increasing your Medicare premiums, which will be taken directly from your Social Security bene-fit. This could resulting in a much lower take home income from Social Security over time.

So, to reiterate what Michael meant by his statement "your income in retirement is based on your income in retirement": the more you earn, the lower the amount that you may actually realize.

As I explained this to my mother, without realizing it, I could see that wooden spoon coming at me at a rate of what seemed like the speed of light, but I was unfortunately frozen still and could only just cringe and take the punishment.

After the tears stopped flowing, I screamed, "What was that for?"

"Why didn't you tell me this before I retired? What am I supposed to do now? HOW COME NO ONE IS HELPING US???!!!" She was beyond reasoning with at this point.

My mother was back to being upset…and rightly so. She had fol-lowed the advice of the financial industry; she delayed paying the tax when she was younger so as to let her investments grow even higher, and later, when she was older and in retirement (now!), she would be in a lower tax bracket and everything would work out wonderfully.

Unfortunately for me, she realized that everything she had done was wrong because the rules were completely changed, and NO ONE had told her. She was now stuck in the position of having to rely on deferred retirement investments, a pension, and Social Security, all of which would be used against her to potentially drive up her Medicare costs. This, in turn, could lower her Social Security benefit and increase her taxes.

To my dismay, this was not the answer mother wanted to hear, and as I assessed the welts on my body, I could hear her asking, as she walked into the kitchen, where she left that wooden fork.

My mother had every right to be upset. She did everything she was supposed to do: She listened to financial pundits who told her to invest in Traditional IRA's because her tax bracket was going to be lower in the future; she pumped up her contributions to her company's 401(k) plan because she was told it was the best option; she didn't take advantage of tax free, and Medicare-penalty exempt investment vehicles because she was never made aware of the problem.

My mother, in the end, became the perfect lemming of the financial industry. She followed exactly what they told her to do, but what they told her didn't stand up to the test of time…and still doesn't. The rules have changed, not because of the markets or economic forces but due to Congressional whims.

In the end, she now realized that everything she had done to prepare herself for retirement, after Congress and our politicians got their way, was wrong.

I quickly tried to calm her down and raise her spirits by informing her about the handful of investment products that were not currently counted as income by Medicare:

- Qualified distributions from Health Savings Accounts
- Qualified distributions from 401(h) plans[30]
- Qualified distributions from Roth accounts (IRA or 401(k))
- Monies from a reverse mortgage

---

30 http://401h.info/

- Income from a cash value life insurance policy
- Certain types of distributions from annuities

Though not college educated, my mom is one smart woman and quickly responded that these were all fine solutions, but:

- Investments into HSAs have to cease once a person accepts Medicare.
- 401(h) plans were something she had never heard of before.
- Roth accounts, which she could see now, are fantastic but have limits on how much a person can invest and wasn't offered through her employer's plan.
- Life Insurance was something she never considered since the financial pundits like Suze Orman and Dave Ramsey stated that permanent life policies that generate cash value were not a good idea.

So the problem, again, was the fact that my mother was trained wonderfully by financial professionals who were probably trying to do what was right; but, as the saying goes, "The path to hell is paved with good intentions."

Her financial plan, which included everything that she had saved and sacrificed in order to make her retirement easier, had just become one of the main reasons why her health care costs would increase and why her Social Security income would decrease.

She learned, just by this third rule, what Michael Gerali was saying: The more income you earn in retirement, the more your Medicare premiums will cost you and the less of a Social Security benefit you will receive since premiums and surcharges are deducted automatically from your Social Security benefit.

And, here is where the potential death spiral begins. Since the Social Security income will be less and less each year, due to Medicare premium increases and/or surcharges , the result is the fact that more and more income will have to be pulled out of financial savings accounts of all kinds, which in turn will be counted as more income, which starts the cycle again.

My mother was, to say the least, not happy. All she could say was, "Why, why didn't anyone tell me, why is this some secret? Are you making all of this up?"

Unfortunately for her and for America's upcoming retirees, I am not making up a single word of this. In fact, this is all on the public record:

The 1st rule—Medicare is mandatory, as we pointed out; and, this is law due to a landmark court case.

The 2nd rule—Medicare is means tested, and this is being shouted from the rooftops by the Centers of Medicare and Medicaid Services (CMS), the group that runs the day to day administration of Medicare and also being preached by the President of the United States, Barack Obama, who has brought this up, not only in his budget for 2014 but also in press conferences as well.

And finally, the 3rd rule-Medicare considers all but a few of your income sources to be includable in their means testing formulas, and this can be confirmed through Social Security, which happens to release this information with every statement they send to every recipient who collects this benefit.

I explained to my mother that I had no idea why the financial industry refuses to broach this subject or even offer the solutions. These are the only reasons I could think of:

- HSAs are tied to health insurance plans and the funds are often spent in the year they are deposited, therefore they escape the attention of many financial advisors. In addition, once a person is enrolled in Medicare they are no longer able to contribute new funds to an HSA account.

- 401(h) plans require that a company sponsor a defined benefit plan. The rules for these plans can be complex and the contributions required can be significant.

- Roth accounts unfortunately have limitations on how much a person can invest in a given year and are not even available to people with higher income levels.

- There is also the Roth 401(k), where a person could invest more, but unfortunately, less than 50% of companies offer it as an option and those that do are only seeing a small portion of employees taking advantage of them.

- As for Roth conversions, where a person makes the decision to change their Traditional IRA to a Roth IRA, the marketing effort by the financial industry has been lukewarm at best. The problems that arise from these conversions are twofold:

  1. There is a tax bill from doing this and a person must pay that tax according to their income bracket on the amount they converted. If a person has $100,000 in a Traditional IRA and converts it to a Roth IRA, and they are in, say, a 25% tax bracket, then they will have to pay approximately $25,000 more in taxes that year.

  2. The tax issue also leads to the fact that if a person decides to pay those taxes by withdrawing money from the $100,000 account, this will hurt the bottom line of the financial professional, as there will be less to invest in the long run. So where is the incentive to market this option?

- Life Insurance is the one financial product that gets beat up the most. As stated earlier by my mother, financial pundits like Suze Orman and Dave Ramsey have been giving listeners reasons to eschew this product for years. For some reason, I cannot figure out why. If we were to just look at history, we could see the value of life insurance.

- 100 years ago in 1913, for some strange reason, Congress decided to establish a permanent income tax:

  - The first permanent income tax we faced was 1% on the first $20,000 earned. It then proceeded to increase incrementally by 1% until a person was paying 7% on $500,000[31].

  - Since 1913, our tax code has exploded from being roughly 164 characters of text, something that could easily be tweet-

31 http://taxfoundation.org/article/us-federal-individual-income-tax-rates-history-1913-2013-nominal-and-inflation-adjusted-brackets

ed or sent via a text, to over 4 million words today. And, the even scarier aspect is we can count on even more to come.[32]

Amazingly, life insurance is the one financial vehicle that has not changed in the last 100 years (maybe because it predates the IRS?!), and I cannot imagine why some financial pundits hate it so much when the following attributes hold true:

- ➢ Life Insurance grows tax deferred.
- ➢ Withdrawals can be income tax free and don't affect Social Security or Medicare taxation.
- ➢ Protects families in case of a tragic loss
- ➢ Generally has guarantees in the form of access to cash values through loans

Yes, there is potential to earn more via investing in the stock market, but returns in the stock market involve lots of risk, and gains are not only taxed by the IRS but lead to the possibility of increased health costs in the form of Medicare premiums and surcharges. This, in turn, can lead to a decrease in Social Security income and a potentially higher tax bill.

Did I mention the fact that even though you may not receive the Social Security benefit you think you should receive, due to Medicare premiums and possible surcharges, you may still be responsible for taxes on that phantom income you never received?

As for writing off your Medicare premiums in retirement, reference the chapter in this book entitled "$100 Billion in lost Medical Expense Deductions". Not only is not knowing this going to affect your health costs, but it will impact your taxes as well. Have you discussed this with your CPA lately?

Conclusion to Rule 3: **Your "income" is almost everything you can think of!**

---

32 http://www.cchgroup.com/wordpress/index.php/press-release/tweet-this-the-modern-income-tax-turns-100-cch-takes-a-look-back-and-ahead/

- Income is practically every source of money you have in retirement.

- Certain types of annuities have tax exclusion ratios that do provide for an amount of income that will be income tax/Medicare tax free.

As I stated before, "Who is helping you plan for this?" Believe it or not, there are a few financial professionals who understand this, and they have taken the time in the pages that follow to detail how they help their clients plan for their health care costs in retirement, while also giving our readers some really interesting ways to address these problems.

But Will This Affect Me?
By Dan McGrath

If you take comfort in thinking that you won't be affected by all of this, consider again my mom's situation.

Mom: "So, what does it matter? I won't be making that much after I retire anyhow."

Me: "Mom, do you remember that 'free money' that the firm contributed to your 401(k) as a company match?"

Mom: "Yes, why?"

Me: "Well, the IRS and Medicare consider almost everything as 'income[33],' so any withdrawal you take from your 401k or IRA Rollover will be subject to state and federal taxes, and for investments not held in the IRA, you may face capital gains taxes, which are based on the increase in value over and above the original investment."

Mom: "Well, I will just live off my Social Security, your father's pension and maybe I'll get a part-time job. There is no need to withdraw any money, so I should be all set."

Me: "Mom, you are forgetting that your Medicare premiums are deducted directly from Social Security income so you will have to make

---

33 http://ssa-custhelp.ssa.gov/app/answers/detail/a_id/1601/~/calculation-of-modified-adjusted-gross-income-%28magi%29

up that difference somehow[34]. You are also forgetting that any wage and pension income will be counted too."

Mom: "But even with the pension, the Social Security and what I will earn from a part-time job that is nowhere near $85,000."

Me: "Yes, but at age 70.5 the federal government requires that you start to withdraw money from those tax deferred accounts."

Mom: "Hmmmm. (Heavy sigh)"

A sad fact of life is that at age 70.5, you must withdraw money from any account that has grown tax deferred, with the exception of money invested into a Roth IRA (This is why they are highly regarded as one of the best investment vehicles available today). The amount you are required to withdraw is a percentage of your total asset base, and each subsequent year the percentage you must withdraw increases. This is not your retirement income plan-it is the IRS's retirement income plan!

And with each increase there is a distinct possibility of edging ever closer to the next income bracket, and higher Medicare premiums.

Retirement is now more about playing defense than it is playing offense, especially for those who will rely on withdrawals from tax deferred accounts for income in retirement.

For calendar year 2013, if you are age 70.5, you must add all your tax deferred account balances from 12/31/12, and divide the total by 27.4, to determine how much money you must take out. **Every dollar** that comes out of an IRA or qualified retirement account is fully taxable as ordinary income. In 2014, the divisor goes down, thus making the withdrawal amount higher, unless the stock market goes down and your retirement accounts shrink in value[35].

This is why some people think the government's stimulus plan is not a great idea for retirees—it keeps pushing the markets higher!

---

34 http://www.medicare.gov/your-medicare-costs/paying-parts-a-and-b/pay-parts-a-and-b-premiums.html

35 http://www.irs.gov/pub/irs-tege/uniform_rmd_wksht.pdf

The Federal Reserve has a recent policy called "quantitative easing"[36]. It is currently lending money to banks and other financial Institutions at very low interest rates. In turn, these financials are investing a lot of this relatively cheap money in the stock market. This, together with regular monthly individual 401(k) investments, is creating large positive flows into the market, and helping stock prices go up.

As the stock market increases, so does the value of retirees' tax deferred accounts. This is a good thing, of course, but when those retirees reach age 70.5, they have to withdraw some amount of that money. And the money that is withdrawn may well be, in effect, doubly taxed.

First, it is taxed as ordinary income at your given tax bracket, as mentioned previously, which may be higher after retirement. Then, if that income pushes you over the Medicare income limits, you will be taxed again in the form of higher premiums, and surcharges.

Given this scenario, here is Mom's likely situation as we look forward:

- Since she is no longer married, the higher income exemption level for married couples is off the table.

- Her house is paid off—so the mortgage interest deduction is gone.

- Her kids are all grown up—so that deduction has gone bye-bye a long time ago.

- Her income:

- She earns roughly $45,000 a year from Dad's pension (60% of his highest three years of earnings).

- She earns roughly $20,000 from Social Security because she retired at age 67, one year past full retirement age after earning roughly $40,000 a year throughout her career.

So her total base income is $65,000.

---

36 http://www.marquetteassociates.com/Research/ChartoftheWeekPosts/ChartoftheWeek/
tabid/121/ArticleID/126/Quantitative-Easing-and-the-U-S-Stock-Market.aspx

Her investments:

- She invested 10% of that $40,000 into a company 401(k), which matched at 6%.

- She invested roughly $2,500 a year for the last 25 years in a traditional IRA.

- She received that 8% Suze Orman rate of return on her investments[37].

- She has roughly $614,000 in total investments.

  - ➤ $431,000 in a 401(k)

  - ➤ $183,000 in a traditional IRA

Mom's total income at the age of 70.5 will be, if everything remains the same, $65k from Social Security income and Dad's pension, along with the amount withdrawn from those tax deferred accounts, which according to that first year formula, will be $22,408, for a total of $87,408. Guess what number she went over that she was sure she wasn't going to have to worry about?

She will pay state and federal taxes on that amount to be sure. But without any tax write-offs, this amount will vault her into that first higher income bracket for Medicare, where she will be taxed again and required to pay extra for Parts B and D of Medicare.

Just think of those high income earners, those really rich people who earned $125,000 a year, maxed out their company's 401(k)s and played the stock market correctly with traditional IRAs because they needed the tax deferral.

Let's say these $125,000 annual earners:

- Are 60 years old

- Plan on retiring at age 70 to max out Social Security

- Invested 10% of their income into their 401(k) at a rate of return of 8%

- Received a 3% company match

37 http://www.womansday.com/life/saving-money/your-ultimate-savings-guide-79739

- Invested $3,000 a year into a Traditional IRA at rate of return of 8%

- Did this for 30 years

- Earned the Social Security maximum amount each year

- Results:

- Their income from Social Security, according to AARP is expected to be: $41,292 annually

- The total amount in their 401(k) = $1,557,644.00

- The total amount in their traditional IRAs = $339,849.00

- Total investments = $1,897,493

- RMD amount from investments upon reaching age 70.5– roughly $69,251

- Total income = $110,543

These fine folks get the privilege of being in the next highest Medicare bracket, so they get to pay approximately 35% more for their Medicare Part B premiums and even more for Part D premiums.

And the super-rich, who will be earning over Medicare's top allowable income level, get to pay an extra 220% on their part B premiums… which will be taken directly from their respective Social Security checks each month.

Conclusion:

Even though you may not consider yourself rich, if you saved and invested during your working years, you may just wind up being considered exactly that when you enroll into Medicare. Moreover, Social Security and investments could bite you when your health is on the line. Welcome to the new retirement.

3

And Your Costs Are ...
by Dan McGrath

M om: "Dear God, what is this going to cost me? How will I pay this the rest of my life? How can anyone plan and prepare for this? I thought I had done all the prudent, responsible things throughout my working life."

Me: "Well, Mom, you will be able to afford it because the premiums and surcharges, if they apply, will be automatically deducted from your Social Security income.[38] So, you really have no choice when it comes to being able to afford them."

Fortunately, for folks who are at or over the age of 65, who are somewhat healthy, and who are already retired, some Medicare costs are not all that onerous.[39]

For purposes of review....

Medicare Part A—This covers hospitalization and is free of monthly premiums as long as you paid in to the system throughout your working career. As with Social Security, as long as you paid into the system for at least ten years, you are eligible for this coverage. But keep in mind that Part A does have serious gaps in its coverage—copays, deductibles, and annual coverage limitations. You can easily cover these costs and fill in the gaps through the purchase of a Medigap policy, also known as a "Med Supp" policy.

38 Congressional Research Service for Congress—Medicare: Part B Premiums June 2013
39 Medicare.gov

Medicare Part B—This covers physician visits. The cost is nationalized, meaning that no matter who you are, how healthy you are, what gender you are, or where you live, you will pay the monthly premium of $104.90 per month or $1,258.80 a year in 2013. Remember from Rule 2 that this premium can be affected if you earn too much income. This coverage also has deductibles, copays, and excess charges which can also be covered completely by a Medigap Policy.

Medicare Part D—This is coverage for prescription drugs. This cost is a little tricky because the premiums depend on where you live, your health, the plan administrator, and your income. This coverage also includes copays and deductibles that cannot be covered by a Medigap policy. The national average according to Q1medicare.com in 2013 was $53.26 a month or $639.12 a year.

Bear in mind that the Medicare Board of Trustees sets a national base premium each year to determine the late enrollment penalties along with the surcharges for high-income earners.

Medigap Plans—These are supplemental insurance programs administered by private health insurers that fill in the gaps of Medicare Parts A and B. The costs depend on residency, type of plan purchased (there are twelve types of plans to choose from), age, and gender.

The average cost of a Medigap policy for a 65-year old male, according to Weiss Ratings, is $175 a month or $2,100 a year. For a 65-year old female, the average cost is roughly $158 a month, or approximately $1,900 a year.[40]

40 http://www.weissratings.com/news/articles/best-medigap-rates/

The chart below shows the base total health insurance costs for a 65-year-old couple in 2013.

Coverage	Male	Female	For Both
Part A	Free	Free	
Part B	$1,258.80	$1,258.80	
Part D	$639.12	$639.12	
Medigap	$2,100	$1,900	
Total	$3,997.92	$3,797.92	$7,795.84

As stated in **the 3 Rules of the new retirement**, Medicare Parts B and D are subject to means testing.[41] This means that the more one earns in retirement, the more one will pay for Part B and Part D premiums. Currently, the income brackets and the surcharges are as follows:

For those earning	For couples	Part B	Part D
$85k <	$170k <	No Penalty	No Penalty
$85k—$107k	$170k—$214k	Premium + 40%	Premium + $11.60
$107k—$160k	$214k—$320k	Premium + 100%	Premium + $29.90
$160k—$214k	$320k—$428k	Premium + 160%	Premium + $48.30
$214k +	$428k +	Premium + 220%	Premium + $66.60

---

41 http://www.medicare.gov/Pubs/pdf/11579.pdf

If they earn even one dollar more than the base limit, that same couple could pay the following:

Coverage	Male	Female	For Both
Part A	Free	Free	
Part B	$1,762.80	$1,762.80	
Part D	$778.32	$778.32	
Medigap	$2,100	$1,900	
Total	$4,641.12	$4,441.12	$9,082.24

The same couple that earns the maximum amount of income as allowed by Medicare and Social Security can expect to pay in 2013 the following:

Coverage	Male	Female	For Both
Part A	Free	Free	
Part B	$4,028.40	$4,028.40	
Part D	$1,438.32	$1,438.32	
Medigap	$2,100	$1,900	
Total	$7,566.72	$7,366.72	$14,933.44

Although Medicare is the least costly coverage on the market today, keep in mind that Part B is automatically deducted from your Social Security check together with any applicable surcharges. What about inflation? How does that factor in?

As explained previously, Medicare Part A is free as long as you have paid into the program over the course of your career;[42] however, the other parts are subject to inflation hikes.

Part B has experienced an average annual inflation rate of 7.856% since its inception.[43] The first monthly premium was issued 47 years ago in 1966 at a cost of $3.00 a month. Today the cost is $104.90.

Part D has experienced an average annual inflation rate of 7.155%.[44] The history of this coverage is not that long (only since 2006), but the

42 http://ssa-custhelp.ssa.gov/app/answers/detail/a_id/400/~/how-to-qualify-for-medicare
43 http://www.ssa.gov/oact/tr/2013/index.html
44 http://www.ssa.gov/oact/tr/2013/index.html

projection from the Medicare Board of Trustees Report of 2012 estimates that the national base premium will increase from $31.17 in 2013 to $54.18 in 2021-that's a 73% boost in only 9 years.

Medigap Plans have risen approximately 4% annually on average. This coverage is determined by age, type of coverage, residency, and the firm administrating the plan. The U.S. Department of Health and Human Services reports that the average inflation rate has been between 3% and 5%.[45]

We can use these inflation rates to calculate what our original couple will pay over 20 years. We will assume they both retire at the age of 65 and earn under the Medicare income limit.

Coverage	Male	Female	For Both
Part A over 20 years	Free	Free	
Part B over 20 years	$56,694.50	$56,694.50	
Part D over 20 years	$26,648.79	$26,648.79	
Medigap over 20 years	$69,438.50	$62,825.31	
Total in retirement	$152,781.79	$146,168.60	$298.950.39

If they earn just a bit more than the Medicare income limit, their costs will be much higher.

Coverage	Male	Female	For Both
Part A over 20 years	Free	Free	
Part B over 20 years	$79,393.92	$56,694.50	
Part D over 20 years	$32,452.88	$26,648.79	
Medigap over 20 years	$69,438.50	$62,825.31	
Total in retirement	$181,285.30	$174,672.11	$355,957.41

45 http://aspe.hhs.gov/health/reports/2011/medigappremiums/index.pdf

And if they somehow earn the maximum amount allowable by Medicare, they will pay the following:

Coverage	Male	Female	For Both
Part A over 20 years	Free	Free	
Part B over 20 years	$181,433.21	$181,433.21	
Part D over 20 years	$59,972.28	$59,972.28	
Medigap over 20 years	$69,438.50	$62,825.31	
Total in retirement	$310,843.99	$304,230.80	$615,074.79

Here's what the numbers will look like for those who are today 60, 55, and 50, and are earning under the Medicare income limit, again assuming a 20 year period of coverage (i.e. They do not live past 85) .

Age	Total Cost Male	Total Cost Female	Total For Both
60	$231,674.16	$222,128.74	$453,802.90
55	$340,491.81	$327,204.04	$667,695.85
50	$491,144.39	$473,080.33	$964,224.71

At an inflation rate of just 5%, the costs will look much different, but they will still be higher than most retirees are planning for.

Age	Total Cost Male	Total Cost Female	Total For Both
65	$132,195.04	$125,581.85	$257,776.89
60	$190,809.12	$181,263.70	$372,072.83
55	$265,617.20	$252,329.43	$517,946.62
50	$361,093.36	$343,029.30	$704,122.66

Me: "Mom, keep in mind that these expenses will eat away at your Social Security income and also at your savings/investment nest egg. The more you have to rely on your own resources, the closer you will get to the income surcharges that Medicare imposes."

You can probably guess how my mom responded to this.

Conclusion

Medicare is going to cost you a lot more than you think.

The historical inflation rates for Medicare are

- Part B—7.856%.

- Part D—7.155%.

- Medigap Plans—between 3% and 5%, and it does depend on your age and your residency, so plan wisely.

Whether these inflation rates will continue at this pace is unknown, but even at a 5% inflation rate, the costs are going to exceed what most retirees have planned for. Importantly, the studies above **do not** include any assumptions for long term care costs that may be encountered before you die! Medicare does not cover most long term care costs.

Certain types of income are not your friend, and if you don't pay attention to this fact, the pain may be extreme over time.

4

How Are Medicare Part B Premiums Determined?

by Michael Gerali

We are often asked where we come up with our numbers when forecasting the future costs of health care. Well, we won't kid you and tell you that it's easy to find out how the government comes up with their figures each year. But if you spend enough time on Google, you can track down the answers most of the time.

First, you need to know that most decisions the government makes are published in the *Federal Register*[46]. Each year toward the end of November, a notice is published in the *Federal Register* that describes the Medicare Part B Monthly Actuarial Rates, Premium Rate, and Annual Deductible. These numbers are important because they form the basis for the actual Medicare Part B premiums that you pay each year.

The Actuarial Rates are broken down into two numbers: the rate for aged enrollees and the rate for disabled enrollees. For example, the 2013 rate was $209.80 for aged enrollees and $235.50 for disabled enrollees.

Now this is where it gets a little tricky…

Medicare uses the actuarial rates to come up with the standard monthly Part B premium. This premium is half of the actuarial rate for enrollees. In the case of 2013, $209.80 * 2 = $104.90.

---

46 www.federalregister.gov

Not bad so far. But because Medicare is now means tested, a different number is used to determine the additional premiums required for those making over a certain amount of income. We will use an example of a single unmarried person earning $100,000 in retirement. Because their income is over the first Medicare threshold bracket of $85,000 but under the second bracket of $107,000, they are required to pay 35% of the total cost of the Part B premium. This 35% is not based on the standard premium or the actuarial rate but on the total cost of Part B. To determine that number, you need to double the aged enrollee actuarial rate. For 2013, that's $209.80 x 2 = $419.60.

So, the total cost for Part B in 2013 is $419.60. If we multiply $419.60 by the means tested percentage in our example, we come up with $146.86 ($419.60 x .35 = $146.86). Medicare now rounds premiums to the closest decimal, so the actual premium would be $146.90 per month for the single retiree in our example; an additional $42 per month.

We can check our math and figures by going to the Social Security website and downloading their publication "Medicare Premiums: Rules for higher-income beneficiaries." It can be found at www.ssa.gov/pubs/EN-05-10536.pdf.

So there you have it. We have removed a little of the mystery of the way the government calculates what it will charge you for Medicare Part B premiums.

One caveat, however: All rules of the government are subject to change!

5

How Are Medicare Part D Premiums Determined?
by Michael Gerali

As a follow-up to the section on how Medicare Part B premiums are calculated, we want to show how the government calculates the Medicare Part D prescription drug premiums. If you thought Part B was confusing, Part D has even more moving parts.

"National average monthly bid amount" is the term used by Medicare to describe the weighted average of the standardized bid amounts for each prescription drug plan. That's a mouthful.

Part D plans are offered by a large number of insurance companies; thus, there is a wide disparity in pricing, depending on the coverage provided by the plan. Unlike Part B, the premium calculated by Medicare for Part D is not the premium you would pay, it is the benchmark used to determine the increased costs for those who enroll in Part D late and for those whose income levels subject them to means testing of their premiums.

In 2013 the average monthly bid amount was $79.64. As a side note, the Centers for Medicare and Medicaid Services (CMS), under the Department of Health and Human Resources, oversee the functioning of Medicare rules and premiums. The annual report for 2013 can be found at the CMS website.[47]

47 Centers for Medicare and Medicaid Services, www.cms.gov/Medicare/Health.../
PartDandMABenchmarks2013.pdf.

Have You Done Algebra Lately?

In the annual report, you will find the formula Medicare uses to determine the Part D base beneficiary premium:

The base beneficiary premium is equal to the product of the beneficiary premium percentage and the national average monthly bid amount. The beneficiary premium percentage ("applicable percentage") is a fraction, with a numerator of 25.5 percent and a denominator that is 100 percent minus a percentage equal to (i) the total reinsurance payments that CMS estimates will be paid for the coverage year, divided by (ii) that amount plus the total payments that CMS estimates will be paid to Part D plans based on the standardized bid amount during the year, taking into account amounts paid by both CMS and plan enrollees.[48]

After performing the analysis above, the base beneficiary premium for 2013 is $31.17.

Now once we know this number, we can then use the formula below to determine the amount of additional premium that is required from those individuals who are subject to means testing. In our example we assume that the single individual is making more than $85,000 and less than $107,000 in retirement income.

It looks like this in its algebraic form:
IRMMA = $31.17 x 35% - 25.5% = $11.61 (rounded to $11.60).

So this individual would be responsible for an additional $11.60 a month for their share of the Medicare means tested Part D premium. This in addition to whatever base premium they pay for Part D.

Penalties

Medicare imposes a late enrollment penalty for those individuals who do not sign up for Part D coverage in a timely manner or have not had creditable Part D coverage on their individual or employer plan.

---

48 ibid

Medicare defines creditable as:

Prescription drug coverage (for example, from an employer or union) that is expected to pay, on average, at least as much as Medicare's standard prescription drug coverage. People who have this kind of coverage when they become eligible for Medicare can keep that coverage without paying a penalty, if they decide to enroll in Medicare prescription drug coverage later and they do not have a gap in coverage of more than 63 days.[49]

Note: High deductible health plans typically do not have Part D coverage that is considered creditable.

Calculating the Penalty

The late enrollment penalty is calculated by multiplying 1% of the "national base beneficiary premium" ($31.17 in 2013) by the number of full, uncovered months you were eligible but didn't join a Medicare Prescription Drug Plan and went without other creditable prescription drug coverage. The final amount is rounded to the nearest $.10 and added to your monthly premium.

This penalty continues with you for the rest of your life and increases as the cost of Part D increases.

More information on Part D penalties can be found at the CMS website.[50]

49 Centers for Medicare and Medicaid Services, www.medicare.gov/part-d/costs/penalty/part-d-late-enrollment-penalty.html.
50 ibid

6

What Happened to My Social Security Check?

By Michael Gerali

How Increasing Medicare Costs Have the Potential to Negatively Impact the Social Security checks of All Americans in the Future

When we think of what is happening with Social Security and Medicare, it reminds us of the nursery rhyme "There was an old lady who swallowed a fly, she swallowed a spider to catch the fly and swallowed a bird to catch the spider." Medicare may soon swallow your Social Security.

Medicare: The Basics

Medicare is made up of four parts.

Part A is the hospitalization benefit that everyone who pays into Social Security for 10 years is eligible to receive at no cost. Those who have paid in for less than 10 years pay a premium of up to $441 a month in 2013.

Part B is the portion that pays for doctors, procedures, and other medical services. You pay a premium for Part B that is based on your income in retirement. The higher your income, the higher the premium you pay. The current minimum cost for Part B in 2013 is $104.90 a month. Often the costs not covered under Part B are offset by purchasing a Medicare Supplement policy (discussed below).

Part C plans are often called Medicare Advantage plans, and are offered by insurance companies whom Medicare pays to take on the liability of parts A, B, and D. These plans are often designed to have lower premiums than Medicare Supplements.

Part D is the Prescription Drug benefit available under Medicare. These plans are typically part of a Medicare Advantage plan or are offered stand-alone for those individuals who purchase a Medicare Supplement plan.

Medicare Supplement plans ("Medigap" plans) are plans offered by insurance companies that offset the deductibles, copays, and out-of-pocket costs not covered under Part A and Part B of traditional Medicare. The plans are standardized and labeled from A to N. The most comprehensive plan is F, which covers everything that Medicare Part A and Part B do not. Because it covers everything, it is traditionally the most expensive plan. Plan K covers the least amount of expenses and is traditionally the lowest priced plan.

Now that you have the basics, let's share some examples of the impact Medicare may have on your Social Security.

What if we told you that a 60-year-old woman today is projected to pay 18.5% of her Social Security check toward Medicare Part B and Part D premiums at age 67? If she starts collecting her Social Security at age 62, that percentage increases to 26%. By age 80 she is projected to pay almost 34% of her Social Security benefit for Medicare. These are not health care costs, but just the premiums required by the federal government and taken directly from her Social Security check.

What can a successful 50-year-old businesswoman expect to pay?

For her, the percentage of Medicare is projected to start at 39% of Social Security income at age 67 and quickly increase to 71% by age 80. When taking potential taxes on Social Security into account, she may find herself writing a check for Medicare that is over and above what she receives in Social Security benefits!

That is correct. Medicare might swallow up all of a successful person's Social Security check. And this is without the threat of means testing Social Security itself!

A new calculator developed by Jester Financial Technologies (JFT) is the first to disclose this little known correlation between Medicare and Social Security.

What many people don't realize is that Medicare is mandatory for those individuals who collect Social Security. If you are still actively working for an employer that has 20 or more employees, then you may be able to delay Part B and Part D coverage until you retire. But when you start collecting Social Security, you will automatically be signed up for Part A coverage. If you start collecting at age 62, then upon turning 65 you are automatically enrolled. What if you change your mind and decide you don't want Medicare? Then you have to pay back all prior benefits from Social Security.

If you have been successful, you will face a new means testing provision which was added in 2003 and which took effect in 2007 that increases the premiums on both Medicare Part B and Part D.

What is means testing?

As shown in Table 1, means testing is where your Medicare premium is determined by your income in retirement. For those individuals who retire at say, age 65, their income is typically calculated by their income tax return two years prior to their retirement. So initially, most people's Medicare premiums in the first year or two come from their income while they were still working. If a single individual earned more than $85,000, then they will most likely pay a higher Medicare Part B and Part D premium. Means testing applies only to the premiums paid for Part B and Part D.

Hold Harmless Clause

Many years ago, Congress enacted the "hold harmless" clause that states that the cost of a Medicare premiums increase cannot exceed the cost-of-living adjustments paid under Social Security that same year. This clause does not apply to those individuals who are subject to Medicare means testing, so their premiums can and most likely will exceed any cost-of-living adjustments provided by Social Security.

Table 1, below, highlights the Medicare means-testing brackets and premiums.[51]

Modified Adjusted Gross Income	Part B Monthly Premium Amount	Prescription Drug Coverage Monthly Premium Amount
Individuals with a MAGI of $85,000 or less Married couples with a MAGI of $170,000 or less	2013 Standard premium = **$104.90**	Your plan premium = **$31.17**
Individuals with a MAGI above $85,000 up to $107,000 Married couples with a MAGI above $170,000 up to $214,000	Standard premium + $42.00 = **$146.90**	Your plan premium + **$11.60**
Individuals with a MAGI above $107,000 up to $160,000 Married couples with a MAGI above $214,000 up to $320,000	Standard premium + $104.90 = **$209.80**	Your plan premium + **$29.90**
Individuals with a MAGI above $160,000 up to $214,000 Married couples with a MAGI above $320,000 up to $428,000	Standard premium + $167.80 = **$272.70**	Your plan premium + **$48.30**
Individuals with a MAGI above $214,000 Married couples with a MAGI above $428,000	Standard premium + $230.80 = **$335.70**	Your plan premium + **$66.60**

---

51 Table 1: Medicare Premiums: Rules for Higher Income Beneficiaries www.medicare.gov

In addition, there are provisions in the 2014 proposed federal budget to increase the number of brackets to 9, along with increasing the premiums on higher income Medicare beneficiaries.[52]

Those proposed changes would take place in 2017. Table 2, below, highlights the potential increased costs[53].

Modified Adjusted Gross Income	Part B Monthly Premium Amount	Prescription Drug Coverage Monthly Premium Amount
Individuals with a MAGI of $85,000 or less Married couples with a MAGI of $170,000 or less	**Projected 2017*** Standard premium = **$131.60**	**Projected 2017 Base Premium*** Premium = **$41.10**
Individuals with a MAGI above $85,000 up to $92,333 Married couples with a MAGI above $170,000 up to $184,666	Means-Tested premium = **$210.60**	Means-Tested premium = **$64.50**
Individuals with a MAGI above $92,333 up to $99,667 Married couples with a MAGI above $184,666 up to $199,334	Means-Tested premium = **$244.80**	Means-Tested premium = **$75.00**
Individuals with a MAGI above $99,667 up to $107,000 Married couples with a MAGI above $199,334 up to $214,000	Means-Tested premium = **$279.00**	Means-Tested premium = **$84.40**
Individuals with a MAGI above $107,000 up to $124,667 Married couples with a MAGI above $214,000 up to $229,334	Means-Tested premium = **$313.20**	Means-Tested premium = **$95.90**

52 THE US BUDGET FOR FISCAL YEAR 2014, page 38
53 Table 2: Medicare Premiums: Projected Medicare Part B and D premiums based on 2014 Federal Budget

Individuals with a MAGI above $124,667 up to $142,333 Married couples with a MAGI above $229,334 up to $284,666	Means-Tested premium = $347.50	Means-Tested premium = $106.40
Individuals with a MAGI above $142,333 up to $160,000 Married couples with a MAGI above $284,666 up to $320,000	Means-Tested premium = $381.70	Means-Tested premium = $116.90
Individuals with a MAGI above $160,000 up to $178,000 Married couples with a MAGI above $320,000 up to $356,000	Means-Tested premium = $415.90	Means-Tested premium = $127.30
Individuals with a MAGI above $178,000 up to $196,000 Married couples with a MAGI above $356,000 up to $392,000	Means-Tested premium = $450.10	Means-Tested premium = $137.8
Individuals with a MAGI above $196,000 Married couples with a MAGI above $392,000	Means-Tested premium = $473.80	Means-Tested premium = $145.10
*The projected premiums utilize historical inflation rates and are for illustrative purposes only.		

Let's take a look at some of the factors that affect both our Medicare and Social Security assumptions.

The historical rate of inflation on Medicare Part B premiums has been 7.85% since its inception in 1966. At the beginning the charge was $3 per month; in 2013, it is $104.90.[54] Figure 1 shows the historical increases of Medicare Part B premiums:

---

54 *Medicare Trustees Report 2012 SMI Cost-Sharing and Premium Amounts, page 229*

Annual Part B Premium

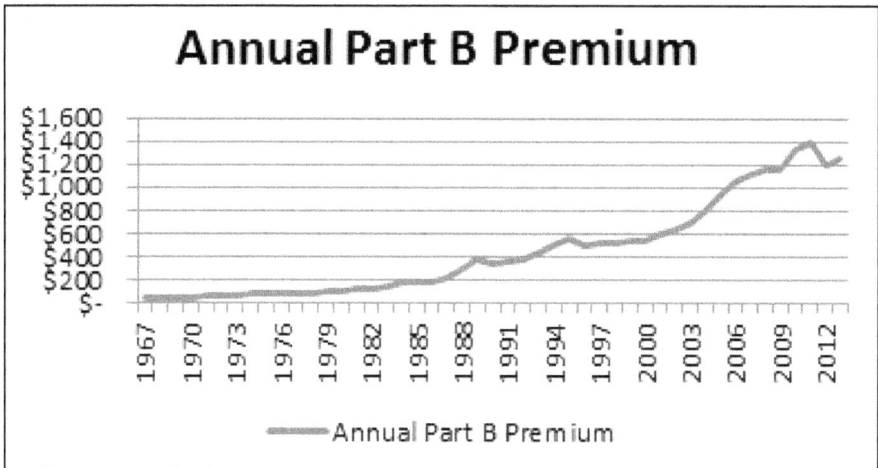

Figure 1: Medicare Trustees Report 2012 SMI Cost-Sharing and Premium Amounts

According to the Medicare trustees report in 2012, the expected rate of inflation for Medicare Part D is 7.15% through 2021.[55]

The proposed 2014 federal budget also introduces the idea of Chained CPI (Consumer Price Index) for calculating the future increases of Social Security. The Congressional Budget Office estimates that a change to the Chained CPI will lower inflation adjustments by .25 basis points over traditional CPI.[56] It has the potential to lower future cost of living adjustments to Social Security. Historically, Social Security retirement benefits have increased at the rate of 4.1% since the addition of cost-of-living-adjustments in 1976 and at roughly 2.5% over the last 20 years.[57] If we assume that the numbers below track their historical counterparts above, we begin to get a clear view of the threat from Medicare.

Jan, age 60, has worked at a manufacturing company her entire career. She found her estimated Social Security benefit at age 67 by visiting the Social Security quick calculator at http://www.socialsecurity.gov/OACT/quickcalc/index.html. Jan could also use the Social Security

55 *Medicare Trustees Report 2012 SMI Cost-Sharing and Premium Amounts, page 229*
56 *http://www.cbo.gov/publication/44088*
57 *http://www.ssa.gov/cola/automatic-cola.htm*

Retirement Estimator, which would give her the most accurate estimate of her future Social Security income (http://www.ssa.gov/estimator/).

Jan found that her projected Social Security income at age 67 is $17,088 annually. We assume her Social Security income will grow at 2.8% annually. Using the JFT calculator, her Medicare Part B and Part D premiums are projected to be $3,174, or 18.5%, of her Social Security income at age 67.

Table 3, below, highlights the projected correlation between her Social Security and Medicare costs. As you can see, her net income is expected to stay roughly level from age 67 to age 90, which won't provide much protection from the effects of inflation.

Age	Year	Social Security Benefit	Part B	Part D	Medicare Premiums	Net Income	Percentage of Income
67	2020	$17,088	$2,137	$1,037	$3,174	$13,914	18.57%
70	2023	$18,564	$2,681	$1,276	$3,957	$14,607	21.32%
75	2028	$21,313	$3,914	$1,802	$5,716	$15,597	26.82%
80	2033	$24,468	$5,712	$2,546	$8,258	$16,210	33.75%
85	2038	$28,091	$8,337	$3,597	$11,934	$16,157	42.48%
90	2043	$32,250	$12,169	$5,081	$17,250	$15,001	53.49%

Table 3: Estimated Social Security Benefit and Part B and Part D Premiums

Now let's switch examples. We have Susan, a 50-year-old married business owner. Susan expects her Social Security income to be $45,624 starting at age 67. For illustrative purposes we assume her husband passes away when she is 62, and she does not remarry. Her planner has estimated that between her future IRA account balance and other investments, she can begin taking $175,000 a year of income at age 67 in addition to Social Security, for a total income of $220,624. This puts her over the current highest Medicare bracket of $214,000 (The 2014 budget provisions would lower the top bracket to $196,000).

Susan's success has added to the cost of her Medicare Part B and Part D premiums. According to the JFT calculator, she can expect to pay $17,855 at age 67 for Medicare. This would be roughly 39% of her Social Security income.

As Table 4 illustrates, by age 80, Susan is receiving $65,329 from Social Security and paying $46,779 in Medicare premiums, or a whopping 71% of Social Security income.

Age	Year	Social Security Benefit	Part B	Part D	Medicare Premiums	Actual Income	Percentage of Income
67	2029	$45,624	$13,509	$4,346	$17,855	$27,769	39.13%
70	2032	$49,565	$16,950	$5,347	$22,296	$27,268	44.98%
75	2037	$56,903	$24,739	$7,554	$32,293	$24,611	56.75%
80	2042	$65,329	$36,108	$10,671	$46,779	$18,550	71.61%
85	2047	$75,001	$52,702	$15,076	$67,777	$7,224	90.37%
90	2052	$86,106	$76,921	$21,298	$98,219	-$12,113	114.07%

Table 4: Estimated High Income Earner Social Security and Medicare Part B and Part D premium: JFT Calculator

This adds up to total Medicare premium costs of $1.14 million to age 90.

What happens if the provisions of the proposed 2014 budget actually go into effect?[58]

Table 5 shows that Susan can expect to pay Medicare premiums of 50% of her Social Security starting at age 67 and 114% by age 85.

---

58 THE US BUDGET FOR FISCAL YEAR 2014, page 38

Age	Year	Social Security Benefit	Part B	Part D	Medicare Premiums	Net Income	Percentage of Income
67	2020	$45,624	$18,153	$4,346	$22,499	$23,125	49.31%
70	2023	$49,565	$22,776	$5,347	$28,123	$21,442	56.74%
75	2028	$56,903	$33,243	$7,554	$40,797	$16,107	71.69%
80	2033	$65,329	$48,520	$10,671	$59,192	$6,137	90.61%
85	2038	$75,001	$70,818	$15,076	$85,894	-$10,893	114.52%
90	2043	$86,106	$103,364	$21,298	$124,662	-$38,555	144.78%

Table 5: Estimated High Income Earner Social Security and Medicare Part B and Part D premiums 2014 Budget: JFT Calculator

These proposed changes would add an additional $300,000 to Susan's Medicare bill by age 90.

Can Susan prepare in advance for this and potentially avoid the Medicare means testing? Based on information from the JFT calculator, if Susan's $175,000 of annual income came from a Roth account, her Social Security and Medicare would look like more like Table 6, below.

Age	Year	Social Security Benefit	Part B	Part D	Medicare Premiums	Net Income	Percentage of Income
67	2020	$45,624	$4,222	$1,931	$6,153	$39,471	13.49%
70	2023	$49,565	$5,297	$2,376	$7,673	$41,892	15.48%
75	2028	$56,903	$7,731	$3,356	$11,087	$45,816	19.48%
80	2033	$65,329	$11,283	$4,742	$16,025	$49,304	24.53%
85	2038	$75,001	$16,469	$6,699	$23,168	$51,833	30.89%
90	2043	$86,106	$24,037	$9,464	$33,501	$52,605	38.91%

Table 6: Estimated High Income Earner with Tax-Free Retirement Income: JFT Calculator

This would reduce the Medicare premium burden to $391,000, or a savings of $750,000 through age 90.

By planning for these scenarios, Susan would be able to significantly reduce her potential Medicare premiums and thereby increase her Social Security income. This is money that she could use to offset the other health care costs in retirement which we have not discussed, such as long term care expenses.

Will this actually happen?

To quote Richard S. Foster, Chief Actuary for Medicare and Medicaid,[59]

"Without unprecedented changes in health care delivery systems and payment mechanisms, the prices paid by Medicare for health services are very likely to fall increasingly short of the costs of providing these services. By the end of the long-range projection period, Medicare prices for hospital, skilled nursing facility, home health, hospice, ambulatory surgical center, diagnostic laboratory, and many other services would be less than half of their level under the prior law. Medicare prices would be considerably below the current relative level of Medicaid prices."

Planning for health care is THE most overlooked component of financial planning.

"There was an old lady who swallowed a horse ... she's dead, of course."

For assistance in calculating your projected health care costs in retirement visit: www.jesterfinancial.com.

---

59 Medicare Trustees Report 2012 SMI Cost-Sharing and Premium Amounts, page 277

7

To Have and to Hold
by Dan McGrath

Mary and John married in 1952, one of 33 million American couples that launched their married life together after World War II and gave rise to the huge baby boom generation. Throughout their six decades together, Mary and John worked hard, lived frugally, and saved regularly. When they retired, they thought they were well prepared to live out their golden years in comfort and security.

Unfortunately, however, John suffered a stroke soon after retiring, and, to say the least, this put a damper on the couple's plans. Mary curtailed her social activities, put their travel plans on hold, and dedicated herself to nursing John through his recovery. But the role of caregiver was a demanding one, and things began to slip. Mary's own health soon began to deteriorate, and the bills began to accumulate.

As was common in their generation, the role of financial manager had fallen to the husband. John had always managed the family's finances and taken care of things like insurance and investments. Mary knew little about such things, and so she sought help from a financial advisor, Fred.

Fred advised Mary to:

- Take a tally of their investments and insurance coverage.
- Locate all important documents, including accounts, insurance documents, wills, trusts and deeds.

- Create a distribution plan to meet anticipated immediate and ongoing needs while mitigating possible tax consequences.

Fred's advice was sound, and if you ever find yourself in a situation similar to Mary's, these are good first steps to take.

But, here is where the advice went astray. Fred advised Mary to cash in the couple's liquid investments first. He explained that by spending taxable monies and leaving tax-deferred investments intact for the present time, the tax-deferred monies could continue to grow and there would be no immediate tax consequences. Fred also suggested that Mary cash in the couple's Roth IRA accounts because there would be no tax consequences for her at this time.

Within a year of his stroke, John passed away, and Mary's financial situation became even more dire. John, unfortunately, did not leave a life insurance policy. His Social Security benefits ceased upon his death[60], and Mary struggled to keep up with ordinary expenses such as utilities, food, and medicine.

Fortunately, she still had those tax-deferred accounts. And, of course, there was the house. But another dilemma arose in that she was not able to tap into the equity tied up in the home.

So Mary found herself in the position of having to liquidate some of the assets in those tax-deferred accounts to help pay for her well-being and home upkeep. Each time she made a significant asset withdrawal, she put herself in a higher Medicare tax bracket and a higher Social Security income bracket.

The IRS taxed Mary's withdrawals as ordinary income[61], and she had no tax write-offs, such as mortgage interest deductions or dependent deductions, to offset this income.

The strategy of deferring taxable income was starting to backfire on Mary. And, on top of that, as mentioned, Medicare viewed her asset withdrawals as income too[62].

---

60 http://ssa-custhelp.ssa.gov/app/answers/detail/a_id/175/session/
L3RpbWUvMTM3OTAxMzIyMS9zaWQvU3dqcWo5QWw%3D
61 http://taxes.about.com/od/retirementtaxes/qt/IRA.htm
62 http://ssa-custhelp.ssa.gov/app/answers/detail/a_id/1601/~/calculation-of-modified-adjusted-gross-income-%28magi%29

Now, instead of being in a Medicare income bracket of $170,000 as a couple, Mary's Medicare tax bracket had been halved, and she was limited to $85,000 before facing surcharges. Over time, her escalating Medicare premiums reduced the amount of her Social Security income and forced her to liquidate more of those tax-deferred assets. Mary was now caught up in a vicious cycle for survival.

Eventually, it became impossible for Mary to afford to stay in her home and she was forced to look at other housing options. Her cherished dream of living out her days in her own home was clearly out of the question. She was faced with trying to qualify for Medicaid, which meant that she would have to give away any remaining assets and her home, and locate a nursing home somewhere in the vicinity of her family.

Until recently, there were adequate housing resources for seniors, especially those with assets. But as baby boomers retire in record numbers and the "Greatest Generation" lives longer, the demand for professional elder care has skyrocketed.

According to the Kaiser Family Foundation, there were 15,622 nursing care facilities in the United States, with approximately 1.66 million beds in 2010. In 2010, only 1.38 million of those beds were occupied.

So today, that leaves less than 300,000 beds available in skilled nursing facilities across the United States. What's more, there is also a growing shortage of health care professionals, including physicians and nurses, to provide elder care in those facilities.

According to the American Association of Medical Colleges[63], there will be a shortage of more than 150,000 doctors over the next 15 years. The "United States Registered Nurse Workforce Report Card and Shortage Forecast,"[64] published in the January 2012 issue of the *American Journal of Medical Quality*, projects a shortage of registered nurses across the country between 2009 and 2030.

Now factor in this assessment from the Centers of Medicare and Medicaid Services' recent 2012 report: According to CMS, roughly 12

63 http://www.aamc.org
64 http://digitalcommons.unl.edu/cgi/viewcontent.
cgi?article=1148&context=publichealthresources

million Americans will need some form of long-term care by 2020. Here is why this is a major problem:

2010 Statistics:

- 15,622 Nursing Care Facilities in the United States
- A total of 1.66 million beds available
- 1.38 million of those beds were occupied

At this rate, there will clearly be a crisis as there will not be enough beds, staff, providers, and/or, possibly, medications to handle the elder population in 2020. This is highlighted by Dr. Peter Kemper's article titled "Long-Term Care Over an Uncertain Future: What Can Current Retirees Expect?" 40% of all Baby Boomers will require LTC for more than 2 years and nearly 25% of those will require that care in a nursing home setting.

The Mary's of the world, due to the current distribution model of financial planning, are in a very difficult situation.

Does this story sound familiar?

Well, it doesn't have to happen to you or your parents. A simple revamp of their distribution plan and some life insurance, coupled with long-term care (LTC) protection and possibly a reverse mortgage, could have changed the course for John and Mary. By modifying the composition and distribution schedule of their assets, and using the equity from their home plus some form of LTC coverage, their story could have read like this:

Before Mary and John retired, they spoke with a financial advisor who placed some of their investments into a long-term care product. They looked at the options, including a standalone policy, a hybrid policy like Lincoln's Money Guard[65] or Pacific Life's Premier Care[66], and an annuity or life insurance product that carried an LTC insurance rider.

65 Https://www.lfg.com/LincolnPageServer?LFGPage=/lfg/lfgclient/fprod/ltc/index.html&LFGContentID=/lfg/lcf/prd/mon/ulpnw
66 http://www.pacificlife.com/PL/Life+Insurance/

This step enabled them to tap into money for long term health care expenses when they needed to.

They investigated a reverse mortgage that enabled them to take the equity out of the home when they needed it. The reverse mortgage allowed Mary to live out her life in the comfort of her own home.

They decided not to follow the mantra of today's financial pundits on buying term life insurance and investing the difference and purchased a small permanent policy on each other, and elected to include a rider for Long-Term Care on these policies, to compliment the other coverage.

They started using their tax-deferred accounts while they were younger, healthier, and in a higher Medicare and income tax bracket.

When John became incapacitated, instead of using their cash, they depleted their tax-deferred accounts while also leveraging the LTC insurance, so they were able to afford in-home professional medical care, and Mary was able to maintain her lifestyle and her health.

When John died, Mary realized less Social Security, but instead of having no options, she had a tax free benefit from the insurance policy on John and the ability to tap into equity from her home through the reverse mortgage. She still had the cash, her investments, and even her Roth IRA while also having access to needed care through her own Long-Term Care policy.

Mary now had multiple assets she could use for income, the option of staying in her home, and the ability to afford to have care provided for her there. And—the last added bonus—her Roth IRAs, the cash settlement from the life policy on John, and the equity from the home were not considered income by the IRS or even Medicare, so her tax bill did not increase, her Medicare premiums remained stable, and her Social Security check did not decline.

By reworking their financial plan, John and Mary were able to have and to hold—and to maximize and augment—their hard-earned assets in an efficient and fiscally responsible way. In essence, they were able to fulfill the vows they took on their wedding day.

8

Medical Expense Deduction: The Lost Opportunity in Retirement
by Michael Gerali

I'm reminded of one of my favorite television shows when I think about the cost of health care in retirement. Jeopardy began in 1964, and the idea has always been to answer a question in the form of a question. So today's question goes like this: What is the amount of deductions that Americans failed to take advantage of in the year 2011? The answer: What is **$100 billion dollars?**

$100 Billion! So how much is $100 billion really?

Well, $100 billion is:

- **The total research and development budget for the U.S. military in 2011, with almost enough left over to fund the medical care of the entire military.**

- **Enough to fully fund the department of agriculture and have $75 billion left over!**

- **Almost enough to fund the majority of the discretionary expenditures of the Department of Health and Human Services.**

- **More than enough money to fund NASA five times over.**

This staggering amount of $100 billion is due to the fact that US taxpayers failed to take basic deductions. Assuming the same percentages going forward, it gets worse; this lost opportunity can grow from $100 billion in 2011 to over $134 billion by 2017.

Why?

The Affordable Care Act of 2010 added a new level of taxation on individuals and retirees. For working individuals, there was an increase in the floor for taking medical expense deductions from 7.5% to 10%. Retirees will see the number increase to 10% beginning in 2017.[67]

What does this mean?

Given that roughly 32% of income tax filers in 2011 itemized their deductions (38% for 65 plus), this means that most people are not taking advantage of deducting their medical expenses while working, or in retirement. For those that do itemize, they lose the ability to deduct the first 7.5% of their expenses.

The Tax Facts

In 2011 there were 145.3 million tax returns filed in the U.S.

- 21.6 million were filed by persons over the age of 65.

- 8.1 million 65 year olds itemized their deductions while 12.8 million took the standard deduction.

- 6.4 million were taxed on their social security income and 4.8 million itemized medical expenses.

- Only 22% of filers over the age of 65 were able to utilize the medical expense deduction.

The total amount claimed was $72.6 billion and the amount in excess of the 7.5% floor was roughly $20 billion. Total income for those over age 65 was $1.343 trillion which means the current floor of 7.5% equals $100 billion. Because of the floor, American's are missing out on billions of dollars in deductions on an annual basis.[68]

---

67 http://www.irs.gov/Individuals/2013-changes-to-itemized-deduction-for-medical-expenses
68 http://www.irs.gov/uac/SOI-Tax-Stats-Individual-Income-Tax-Returns-Publication-1304-(Complete-Report)#_download

How this affects the average American

According to 2011 data from the Bureau of Labor Statistics, the average out-of-pocket health care expenditure was $5,028 for persons 65 and older. If you add in Part B at $104.90 per month, this totals an annual amount of $6,287 spent on health care. Assuming a 20% tax bracket, the lost income is $1,257 a year, which is enough to pay the average cost of both out-of-pocket medical services and supplies. In a 30% bracket, this totals approximately $1,886, or enough to pay out-of-pocket medical services and supplies, along with prescription drug costs.[69]

To put this in context, the average mortgage deduction taken by Americans over the age of 65 in 2011 was $8,712. Based on this, average medical expenses are 72% of the average home mortgage deduction for this group.[70]

Would your accountant or your financial professional advise you to avoid taking the home mortgage deduction, if you were eligible?

Unfortunately, the problem will get worse.

Medicare premiums have increased at slightly under 8% since their inception in 1966. If this pace continues into the future, the average Medicare Part B premium will increase from $104.90 a month today to over $475 a month in 20 years.[71]

In addition, there are various means testing proposals put forth in the 2014 budget and by other advocacy groups that would further increase the means testing costs for those Americans with higher incomes in retirement. In fact, the stated goal is to increase means testing until 25% of retirees pay an additional cost above the basic premium today of $104.90 a month.[72]

---

69 http://www.bls.gov/cex/ce_midyear_announce.htm

70 Source: U.S. Census Bureau, Current Population Survey, 2012 Annual Social and Economic Supplement.

71 http://bipartisanpolicy.org/blog/2013/05/reducing-subsidies-higher-income-medicare-beneficiaries

72 http://bigstory.ap.org/article/ap-newsbreak-medicare-means-test-plan-detailed

So what can a person do to take advantage of this deduction in retirement?

One place to start is by looking at the benefits provided by your employer, and then other options that are available to you. When you evaluate them based upon the need to lower your health care costs in retirement, you may see many of these in a different light.

9

The Three Holy Grails of Health Care Planning

by Michael Gerali

Why You Should Be Knocking Down the Door of
Your Advisors and Employer to Find Out More!

Once upon a time in America, government and companies alike took care of the needs of their employees by providing generous benefit packages that provided pensions and health care benefits. Since the 1980s, these benefits began to disappear in the private marketplace. The recent bankruptcy declaration by the city of Detroit is an acknowledgement that soon many governments may no longer be able to honor the promises they made to their retired and current workforce.

The biggest threat is to the health care benefits provided to employees and retirees. The majority of these benefits are unfunded (i.e. no plan has been established that holds assets to pay these future liabilities) and not constitutionally guaranteed in many states. Even if there is a state constitutional "guarantee", it may not hold up to the judgment of the U.S. Supreme Court. We will all learn more in the next few years as employees and unions alike have challenged Detroit's bankruptcy.

Whatever the outcome, this much is clear. The good ole days are gone and with them the notion that your employer is going to take care of you in retirement. Employees must now begin to plan for their own retirement and ensure they make the best use of their money while working, as well as in retirement. One of the best ways they can do that is to maximize the use of the state and federal tax code to leverage and sustain their retirement dollars.

First Holy Grail

Voluntary Employee Benefit Association (VEBA)[73]

Created in 1928, VEBA's are tax-exempt associations that allow employers and employees to set aside money for the purpose of funding health care benefits while working and in retirement. These contributions are tax deductible to both the employer and the employee. In addition, the benefits grow tax deferred and can be withdrawn for health care expenses on a tax-free basis. Veba's are most often found in the governmental marketplace, although General Motors utilized a VEBA when they funded the health care benefits of their retirees in 2007 before they declared bankruptcy in 2009. (No, we're not picking on Michigan!)

If given the opportunity, an employee cannot find a better place to save for health care benefits than participating in a VEBA. Often when discussing VEBA options with employees, the suggestion is made that investing in a 403(b), a 401(k), or a 457 plan is a better option. While there are few absolutes in life, the tax-deductible contributions and tax-free distributions of a VEBA make it a far superior vehicle for funding retirement health care costs (all things being equal; i.e., investment returns).

In addition, distributions from a VEBA do not constitute income as currently defined under the Modified Adjusted Gross Income calculations.[74] There will be more information regarding this to follow.

---

73 Internal Revenue Service, *http://www.irs.gov/irm/part7/irm_07-025-009.html*
74 Social Security Administration,http://ssa-custhelp.ssa.gov/app/answers/detail/a_id/1601/~/calculation-of-modified-adjusted-gross-income-(magi)

Second Holy Grail

Health Savings Accounts (HSA)[75]

HSAs were approved by Congress in 2003 and became available to the public beginning in 2004. To participate in an HSA, an individual is required to own a health insurance policy that is considered a high-deductible health plan (HDHP). The HDHP cannot provide first dollar coverage, with the exception of preventative care. The minimum deductible is $1,250 for an individual and $2,500 for a family. For 2013, the maximum contribution that a single individual can make to the HSA on a tax-deductible basis is $3,250. For a family, the maximum deduction is $6,450. There is also a $1,000 catch-up contribution that can be made by individuals over the age of 55.

Why HSA?

Since not all employers offer HDHP plans, you should encourage your employer to investigate adding them as an option if they don't currently. Conventional wisdom would encourage an HSA account holder to use the funds inside of their HSA to pay for out-of-pocket health care costs while they are working. However, once you understand the hurdles facing us all in retirement, it may make sense for many individuals and their families to accumulate money inside their HSA. Like a VEBA, the HSA account allows the holder to take money from the account tax-free as long as it is used for qualified medical expenses.[76]

Again, there is no better vehicle than one that is tax deductible, tax deferred, and tax free upon distribution. In addition, most people will have an easier time finding access to a HDHP and HSA combination than a VEBA.

---

75 Internal Revenue Service,http://www.irs.gov/publications/p969/ar02.html
76 Internal Revenue Service,http://www.irs.gov/publications/p502/

Third Holy Grail

401(h) Accounts[77]

While this is the least available account for purposes of funding health care costs, it may just be the best for those who would like to fully fund the cost of their health care in retirement. The 401(h) account is a sub-account of a defined benefit pension plan. There are three types of defined benefit pensions (DB): defined benefit, cash balance, and money purchase. Each one can include a 401(h) account for the purposes of funding health care costs in retirement. These plans allow only new contributions going forward, not retrospective contributions. The maximum limit that can be allocated to the 401(h) account is 25% of the total contributions made to the plan. Defined Benefit plans are typically utilized to assist employees who have underfunded their retirement plan in catching-up by making larger tax-deductible contributions. Cash balance plans are often more flexible than traditional DB plans and offer a great opportunity to maximize deductions and fund for health care. Like our first two grails, distributions from the 401(h) account are tax free when used to pay for medical expenses. The contributions going into the 401(h) provide an excellent opportunity for health care funding and can allow individuals to accumulate 10s, if not 100s, of thousands of dollars in his or her account. Ideal candidates for these plans are employers with existing defined benefit plans, along with those with profit sharing or 401(k) plans that make safe harbor or large matching contributions to their employee's accounts.

So there you have it. If your advisor, accountant, or employer has not discussed these options with you, then they are allowing you to miss out on what is arguably the best investment vehicle to fund future health care costs.

If these are not enough reasons, there might be one more that should be considered, the "Grand Daddy" of them all.

---

77 Internal Revenue Service, *www.irs.gov/pub/irs-tege/chap801.pdf*

Modified Adjusted Gross Income (MAGI)[78]

This is the income that is used when determining whether an individual is subject to means testing of their Medicare premiums. The more money an individual earns in retirement, the higher the potential Medicare premiums paid. Today, a person in the highest bracket, $214,000, pays a Medicare premium for Part B that is 220% of that for someone who earns less than $85,000.[79] In numerical terms, the lowest Part B premium is $104.90 and the highest is $335.70. Although distributions taken from a DB plan are taxable, those taken from the 401(h) account are not. The 401(h) distributions are also not part of the MAGI calculation, thus avoiding an increase in a person's income and potentially avoiding the higher Medicare premiums.

Distributions from the VEBA and the HSA also don't count towards the MAGI calculation.

If this doesn't seem like a lot, tell that to a 50 year old. If he lives to age 90, he can expect to pay a difference of $873,413 between the lowest and highest Medicare means testing brackets over his lifetime, based on historical rates of inflation.[80] Even if Medicare increases at only 6% annually, the difference is still more than $517,811 between the highest and lowest income brackets.

For assistance in calculating your projected health care costs in retirement, visit www.jesterfinancial.com.

---

78 Internal Revenue Service, http://www.irs.gov/Businesses/Small-Businesses-&-Self-Employed/Passive-Activity-Loss-ATG-Exhibit-2.2:-Modified—Adjusted-Gross-Income-Computation
79 Social Security Administration, *www.ssa.gov/pubs/EN-05-10536.pdf*
80 Jester Financial Technologies 2013, Health Care Calculator

10

Hey Mom, Can We Talk?
A Financial Planner's Appeal
to His Mother

by Robert Ryerson

ey, Mom, can we talk? There are some changes that affected the Social Security and Medicare programs in recent years that you will need to know about so you won't be blindsided in 5–10 years when you retire. It's boring but important stuff. The Medicare Prescription Drug, Improvement, and Modernization Act (MMA) of 2003 gave us prescription drug coverage under the big Medicare umbrella for the first time, but it also introduced means testing for Medicare Part B and D premiums. The Affordable Care Act, otherwise known as "Obamacare," added some new taxes to the picture as well, and the president's current budget proposal (for 2014)recommends further increases in costs associated with Medicare premiums. Beginning in 2017, the Budget proposes to "restructure "income-related premiums under Parts B and D by increasing the lowest income-related premium by five percentage points, from 35% to 40%, and also increasing other income brackets until capping the highest tier (that is, what you pay) at 90% of your Part B premium.[81]So, despite the government repeatedly trying to convince the rapidly maturing Baby Boomers that they are going to keep Medicare "as we know it," the truth is we just lost Medicare "as we knew it." As the tidal wave of

81 http://www.whitehouse.gov/omb/budget

baby boomer demand swamps the system, the outlook for price increases on Medicare supplement plans and long-term care insurance policies
is also not encouraging, and, frankly, the history of price increases, or
"inflation" tied to all aspects of Medicare and long-term health needs
speaks for itself. According to the Heritage Foundation's May 2013 Back-
grounder #2801 report,[82] in addition to these significant upcoming cost
increases, senior citizens' access to care is likely to get worse as well as
mandated cuts in Medicare's payments for services to many providers
will fall below the providers' costs, forcing them to withdraw from serv-
ing Medicare patients without some special relief from the politicians.

Mom, it's actually right there in the latest presidential budget, under
the stated goal of "improving the financial stability of the Medicare program by reducing the federal subsidy of Medicare costs for those beneficiaries who can most afford them." Isn't that a nice way of warning you
that you are going to get pick pocketed in the future? By the way, you
don't find this plan for greatly increasing the amount of people who will
be affected by these higher monthly Medicare premium costs under the
"Social Security" section (pages 167-168) of the Budget proposal, no.
And you don't find this bad news about proposed higher costs for retirees under the "Health and Human Services" section (pages 93-101). No,
instead you find this alarming news under a section entitled "Reducing
the Deficit in a Smart and Balanced Way"(pages 35-46)! Seriously. Why
is this happening? Because the federal social programs system is going
broke, and the tidal wave of rapidly aging Baby Boomers will only make
the situation worse. The states are all struggling with Medicaid costs
they cannot afford as well. For people who don't plan ahead in this new,
tougher environment, there is a real risk that they will unintentionally
go through a huge amount of money, or be forced to spend down their
asset base, and accidentally impoverish their spouse or disinherit their
kids before they die—none of which they wanted to do, of course. The
states are getting more aggressive, too, because they desperately need
money. There are 29 states that have "filial responsibility" laws on the

---

82 http://www.heritage.org/research/reports/2013/05/the-obama-medicare-agenda-why-
seniors-will-fare-worse

books that could, in theory, be used to pursue, or obligate adult children to provide financial assistance to a needy parent. ABC News reported on May 23, 2012 that the Superior Court of Pennsylvania (one of two intermediate appellate courts in Pennsylvania) upheld a verdict against a 47 year old man they found liable for his ill mother's $93,000 nursing home bill under their "filial responsibility" law!

The Gift of the MAGI (to the government, that is!)

Under these new rules, a high-income earner will potentially face a Medicare surtax, Medicare premium surcharges, and Medicare Supplement plan surcharges.[83] We in the retirement planning community already know that the costs of premiums on long-term health care insurance policies need no help from the government to rise. The market and the insurance companies already have that situation well in hand, Mom. More importantly, the money that you take out of your 401(k) or IRA accounts will now count, along with your Social Security, pension, tax exempt interest, capital gains, interest, and dividends, toward something the government calls your "Modified Adjusted Gross Income," or MAGI. It is this "MAGI" that all the new increases are based on, and a good part of these increased expenses will be deducted right out of the your Social Security benefit before you get to spend a penny. So it will take some new ways of looking at things in terms of longer term planning if you are to avoid lots of potentially unnecessary expenses and taxes.

Mom, here are some interesting stats. According to a recent study by MetLife's Mature Market Institute, 52% of those baby boomers born in 1946 are fully retired, and 86% of those born in 1946 are collecting Social Security, but 43% said they actually began collecting earlier than they had planned to.[84] Less than 25% of these folks have long-term care insurance.

If Medicare premiums, deductible, copays, and supplement plans are already consuming on an average of 25% of retirees Social Security ben-

83 http://www.whitehouse.gov/omb/budget
84 https://www.metlife.com/assets/cao/mmi/publications/studies/2013/mmi-oldest-boomers.pdf

efit, according to the Met study, how will these people react when that percentage approaches 50%? You may say, but wait a minute, what about all the cost of living adjustments (COLAs) I'm going to get on my Social Security after I'm retired? Well, I didn't say you'd lose a large chunk of your Social Security benefit to these costs right away. It is going to occur over time, but if we look out far enough, and we study the recent historical recent trends regarding Medicare premium increases versus COLAs received, we can see that if you live to your life expectancy or beyond, this will become a serious issue for many retirees. If these retirees were not counting on yielding upwards of 50% of their expected Social Security benefits for Medicare costs, where will they get that extra money? If the answer is they'll have to pull it from their qualified retirement plans, we've got some more problematic news for them (more on this a little later).

Of course, most financial advisors are not talking to their clients about these health care cost problems because they are unaware themselves, so I think your friends, unfortunately, stand a good chance of receiving **traditional** planning or investment advice, which does nothing to address these upcoming risks and expenses, and which may actually make things worse.

Ways to Skin the Income Cat

One thing that should be clear right away, Ma, is the fact that you and most people are going to need more income in retirement than they thought they were going to, because they are likely going to be netting less every month from their Social Security checks and paying more in several other places. So, what are some ways to generate that extra needed income in the future?

Can dividend paying stocks or mutual funds do it?

Yes. In fact, over very long periods of time, dividend-paying stocks can give you great returns.

Can rental real estate do it?

Yes. You may or may not wish to be a landlord (you can always hire a property manager if you don't want to be an active landlord), but depending upon the property, you may have nice steady yields from this strategy as well.

Will a reverse mortgage do it?

Yes. Many retirees have negative preconceived notions about reverse mortgages because they think they will disinherit their heirs over time by eating up the home's equity. But what is the difference if they "unintentionally" deplete liquid assets or illiquid equity in a home in order to maintain their lifestyle, or to respond to increases in their living expenses over time? There is actually a good deal of flexibility to reverse mortgages, and they should be considered as one more viable arrow in the future income quiver. Most importantly, the "income" one receives from a reverse mortgage is not considered income by the IRS, states, Social Security, or Medicare means testing (MAGI), so it can help keep your potential Medicare premium costs lower while simultaneously providing the funds needed for ongoing expenses.

Can bonds or bond funds do it?

Yes. In fact, that's what bonds are for, historically. This is not an easy choice, however, because there is a myriad of bonds and a myriad of factors involved in terms of whether they are an attractive or appropriate choice for income production. However, since bonds are interest rate sensitive, and since interest rates are near historic lows at this time, Warren Buffett is suggesting that bonds come with a warning label for investors!

Can Real Estate Investment Trusts do it?

Yes. REITs were also designed for income purposes, but like bonds, there are lots of different types, and lots of different risk levels to consider.

Can CDs and T-bills, and savings bonds do it?

Yes, but not so easily today. The yields on so-called riskless invest-ments are so low that you are almost forced to look elsewhere if you have a defined income need. Historically, these were always solid, safe, convenient choices, but if interest rates stay low for a prolonged peri-od, they will not do the trick for you for income production purposes, and will not preserve your purchasing power against inflation. We keep expecting to see higher rates, but that may not happen for a while. The retirees in Japan have had horribly low rates for 23 years now, and are still waiting, for example.

Will private guaranteed pensions/lifetime income annuities contracts do it?

Yes. Along with Social Security, these should be a fundamental item in your long-term income plan, especially if you will not receive a pen-sion from your employer upon retirement. Annuities sometimes get some bad press, but the truth is that annuities can help address several longer term risks, and do so in a guaranteed fashion. In fact, a simple lifetime income annuity—a "private pension," if you will—can take all the following risks off the table simultaneously:

- Reinvestment Risk
- Deflation Risk
- Order of Returns Risk
- Market (principal) Risk
- Longevity Risk (this one magnifies all the others)

These days, there are annuity contracts that not only guarantee you a future stream of income that you cannot outlive, but which also have inflation or long-term care riders built in to boot. Since almost all of these lifetime income annuities allow the contract holder to decide when to turn on the tap, so to speak, there is a measure of flexibility or control that can help on the longer term Social Security and Medicare premi-ums planning front as well. You probably remember, Mom, that with

IRAs and 401(k)s there is no flexibility or control. Once you reach age 70 ½, the "required minimum distributions" rules dictate when and how much fully taxable money you must withdraw. These required minimum distributions are also counted as income under the MAGI rules, and can cause you to pay more every month for Medicare premiums all by themselves. The older you get, the more money you will have to take out, and the better the chance that you'll hit these higher Medicare premium levels. This means that they'll be taking more and more money directly out of your Social Security benefit every month. Now we can maybe assume that 20 years into retirement, you may not be as active as you were when you first retired, but shouldn't we definitely assume that everything will cost a lot more in 20 years anyway? So again-where is all this extra needed income going to come from, and does the source matter that much? Yes, it does! If the income that lands on the MAGI schedule is not the kind we want, then to the extent you can plan ahead and avoid making the "bad income" situation worse , that is a sound strategy. The problem is that all of the income sources I discussed previously will fall onto the MAGI/bad income side of the equation (of course, there is no "bad" income in retirement-I'm just trying to use that word to highlight the implications under the "new retirement rules").

In fact, if you have a large amount of money in a tax-deferred retirement plan, once your RMDs really start to kick in (they're not too painful in the first few years), the odds are good that your MAGI may rise to a level that puts you into the surcharge brackets, as mentioned previously. This means a larger percentage of your Social Security check will be eaten up before it gets to your bank account, which in turn, over time, may force you to draw down more and more money from sources that will further increase your MAGI. It is a cycle we need to plan on avoiding, if possible, by taking some intelligent steps now.

Perhaps the best and most readily available sources of "good income" or income that doesn't count toward your MAGI, are loans from a cash value, or "permanent" life insurance policy. In fact, the annual income from a cash rich life insurance policy doesn't even show up on a 1099 for the IRS or state to tax. The loans never have to be paid back-they are intentional loans we are using for tax free income in retirement. It is true that the loans will reduce your death benefit over time, but if we choose a policy that grows your death benefit during the contribution phase, then you are really just giving back some of that growth as you take the income out, and using it on yourself for a tax free retirement supplement.

Sure, there has to be a need for the life insurance, but how many single or married people cannot use life insurance to protect or enhance the lives of people they care about when they are gone? When we think about using life insurance as a wealth management tool, because we recognize that it has several features and benefits that qualified plans simply do not, then the case is made even stronger. Almost everyone should have some permanent life coverage.

Frankly, and I realize that this may sound controversial because of the way we've all been trained to think about deferred qualified plans the past 30 years or so, I think the scales are actually tipped pretty clearly on the side of life insurance when we do a head to head comparison with qualified plans:

Qualified Plans[85] vs. Whole Life Insurance Plans[86]
A Comparative Look

Qualified Plans	Whole Life Insurance
Funds protected from creditors	Funds protected from creditors
Contribution limits and anti-discrimination testing	Funding not limited based on income and no anti-discrimination rules or tests
Annual filing requirement and administration costs (in the thousands)	No annual filing or administrative costs
Contributions made with **pre-tax** dollars (taxes are "postponed")	Premiums paid with after tax dollars

---

85 Including 401Ks, 403Bs, Pensions, Profit Sharing Plans, 457 Plans, Traditional IRA
86 Non Direct Recognition Whole Life Insurance Policies

Earnings grow tax deferred	Cash values grow tax deferred
Requirement Minimum distribution rules in effect at age 70 ½ (mandatory taxable income)	No Required Minimum Distribution rules (no requirements relating to timing or amounts)
Withdrawals after age 59 ½ are fully taxable by feds and state as ordinary income (1099 is issued)	Withdrawals (taken as policy loans) are **free** from federal and state taxes (no 1099 is issued)
Withdrawals taken under age 59 ½ are fully taxable and subject to a 10% additional penalty tax	Withdrawals taken under age 59 ½ (as policy loans) are **free** from federal and state taxes and do not face the 10% penalty tax
All withdrawals generate a 1099	Withdrawals do not generate a 1099
Can affect taxation of Social Security benefits	Loans do not affect taxation of Social Security benefits
Can affect means testing of Medicare premiums B & D	Loans do not affect Medicare premiums for means testing
Does not include any rider or tax free access for long term care or chronic illness	Chronic illness/Long Term Care riders built into policy at no cost—tax free funds available
Can transfer to spouse tax free at death, but all dollars are then taxable as the spouse uses them. Cannot transfer tax free to children	Tax free transfer (death benefits) to spouse or children
Loan provision limited to $50,000, if available	Guaranteed loan provision—Loans not limited to any particular amount—generally up to 80%—85% of cash values

Money taken out for loans does not participate in earnings or appreciation	Money taken out for loans continues to accrue dividends and interest
Loans not forgiven at death—become taxable to estate	Loans are forgiven at death and subtracted from death benefit which remains tax free
Loans must be paid back over the next 60 months	Loans are unstructured and do not have to be paid back on any set schedule
May be subject to AMT	Not subject to AMT
A disability likely means no more contributions to your retirement plans	A policy with a disability waiver means the insurance company pays the premium if you are disabled, and completes the plan for you, to age 65
Withdraws during down markets may affect longer term income potential	Guaranteed loan provision provides income options and flexibility in down markets
Potential superior long term returns (with risk , however)	No loss provisions—no market risk (moderate returns)

Due to increasing life expectancies, we planners are now told to have people look at and plan for a 30-year period of time (or more) in retirement. If this is the case, will an income plan that looks reasonable or comfortable at age 66 or 70 still be okay at 80 or 85? Of course not. That's why, in addition to those income producing vehicles mentioned above, many advisors believe it is actually dangerous not to have any exposure to growth stocks or hard assets or real estate holdings-asset classes that have historically been able to keep pace with inflation better than CDs or other fixed income investments. For people who are completely risk adverse, and whom we cannot convince to have these exposures in their overall portfolios, we try to let them know candidly that they may need to deplete some of their capital base down the road if inflation becomes a problem or if they live beyond their life expectancy. There is no magic bullet that can protect their purchasing power over time without some risk. They must be able to tolerate some fluctuations.

Summing it up

Mom, I've never done this in all the years I've been in this business, but these changes are so important and will take so many people by surprise, that I'm asking you to let me meet with all your friends to discuss these issues. Left to their own devices, they are likely to procrastinate or face inertia or even bewilderment at the implications of these upcoming changes.

I can tell you that all of your friends and their spouses are currently counting on all of their projected Social Security benefits and maybe some cost-of-living increases before they get there. And they are already mentally using those numbers in their thoughts about retirement. It's only natural. What they are not thinking about is that once they are in retirement, a larger and larger portion of their Social Security check and any cost of living adjustments, will be diverted toward Medicare premiums. They are not aware of the new changes and costs they'll be facing down the road in just a few years, and they almost certainly not aware of how persistent and brutal the inflation rate has been on the Medicare premiums and Med Supp fronts over time.

The good news, Mom, is that they are still in the right age range to be able to implement some important long-range strategies that will help them survive these problems and have a secure, comfortable retirement. They really do need to hire a team of professionals, however, who are aware of and comfortable with these big changes and who know how best to address them. As I mentioned earlier, the vast majority of advisors, unfortunately, are still recommending traditional courses of action that can actually hurt the retirees down the road by making more of their money susceptible to the surcharges and higher tax formulas. These advisors are unaware of the new laws, and the alarming trends that recent proposals imply for their clients. So I hope you understand why I feel it is so critical that my team reviews everyone's current and projected situations and recommends appropriate steps to head these problems off at the pass.

Here are the main points to keep in mind:

- We are in some strange and rapidly changing waters. With very few exceptions, it is imperative for pre-retirees and recent retirees to hire qualified advisors to help them navigate successfully and efficiently. Many tried and true planning strategies will no longer be the most cost efficient ways to go.

- Since you will very likely need more income than you originally thought in retirement, due to these changes in your future Medicare and health care costs that we've been discussing, the focus of at least a decent portion of your portfolio should be on building or locking in some future income streams.

- Although there is a small percentage of the population that may be able to research, integrate, and implement their estate and long-term health care planning, income planning, tax planning, and investment planning efficiently and appropriately by themselves, for the vast majority of people, this is not a do-it-yourself proposition.

- There are lots of ways to generate sustainable income in retirement—from utilizing vehicles with no risk to principal, all the way to vehicles with plenty of risk to principal. The important thing to keep in mind is that not all income sources are now equal under the new Affordable Care Act/Medicare paradigm. Although CDs, bonds, dividends, and forced distributions from IRAs will all help you bring in income, they will also all count toward your Modified Adjusted Gross Income. Certain annuity income streams, cash value life insurance policy income streams, and reverse mortgage income streams, however, will avoid being counted toward your MAGI.

- Since people are living longer, and it is a reasonable assumption that there are more life-extending breakthroughs coming in the world of science and medicine, retirees and pre-retirees cannot forget about the importance of trying to preserve or maintain the purchasing power of their future income streams. Adding inflation riders to financial vehicles that offer them, and intentionally owning some precious metals, natural resources, and/or real estate (i.e., "hard assets") in your portfolio is imperative, and could mean the difference between a comfortable or uncertain longer term retirement outlook.

11

Why Is My Financial Adviser Recommending an Annuity?

by Robert Klein

efore we dive into why one would buy an annuity to solve the health care and Medicare crisis, let's take a moment to define what an annuity is. According to *Investopedia*, "an annuity is a financial product sold by financial institutions which is designed to accept and grow funds from an individual and then, upon annuitization, pay out a stream of payments to the individual at a later point in time. Annuities are primarily used as a means of securing a steady cash flow for an individual during their retirement years."[87]

I like to define an annuity in simpler terms. An annuity is simply a contract from an insurance company that is the opposite of life insurance. Life insurance solves the problem if you die prematurely. Your heirs are left with money so they are not destitute. The rent or mortgage is paid. There is money for food. Maybe there's enough for your kids to go to college. Possibly even enough to pay for a really nice wedding or two. Whatever your priorities are, life insurance creates a lot of liquidity after you pass away-tax free.

Annuities solve the problem if you live too long. Money can be paid out as needed, or the owner of the annuity can exchange the annuity for what *Investopedia* mentions above: *annuitization*. Annuitization is a

87 http://www.investopedia.com/terms/a/annuity.asp

technical term for creating a pension type stream of income. You can request an annuitization for periods as short as five years or as long as you live. Should you take out money periodically or should you annuitize? Well, that depends on your specific situation.

So why would you want an annuity if you can create your own tax shelter using a qualified retirement plans, such as 401(k)s, 403(b)s, and IRAs? Why are you buying an immediate income annuity when rates are low (e.g., 2009–2013) when you can do better with the income from dividends and interest from certain bonds?

The confusion with annuities, for the general public, the financial writers, and even some financial professionals is that they still view annuities as investments. While some academics and self-regulatory organizations such as FINRA and the SEC may agree, they miss the main reason why annuities exist in the first place—income! You are buying an income stream now or in the future. If only we can change the name of what the product/solution is…. but, I digress.

Eve Kaplan is a fee-based advisor in New Jersey and a contributor to *Forbes*. She lists nine reasons to avoid variable annuities. Ms. Kaplan cites an example with an annuity that was presented to her father: "I regularly receive e-mails from annuity firms who promise substantial commissions for selling annuities (note: they don't know I don't sell products). My 84-year-old father is a great example of a potential variable annuity victim—a financial advisor tried to sell him a variable annuity a few years ago, when he was 79. My father showed the proposal to me—the surrender period was 10 years and the fees were well over 3% per year. My father would not have been able to access this annuity without penalty until he turned 89."[88]

If you read her article, she leaves you with the impression that those who sell annuities are misleading the public. I'm not saying all salesmen are always truthful, but she's confusing a surrender charge with liquidity. Most annuities that do not pay out income right away will allow a por-

---

88 http://www.forbes.com/sites/feeonlyplanner/2012/07/02/9-reasons-you-need-to-avoid-variable-annuities/

tion of your original deposit out each year without a penalty, provided you don't go over the allotted percentage. It is stated in the prospectus and marketing literature. Ms. Kaplan is only talking about variable annuities, which are just one type of annuity. I'm not going to say they are greatest thing since slice white bread, but they do have a place for those planning for income in retirement and income to overcome potential health care expenses.

Another interesting comment comes from a well-respected financial journalist at *Forbes*, Janet Novack. She argues that most retirees don't need annuities because they have other potential income sources, such as a 401(k) or IRA. Plus, she says most already own an annuity—Social Security.[89] Well, Social Security can be thought of as an annuity. However, you will see how dangerous it is to rely on Social Security, IRAs, and 401(k)s for income. That danger is not just losses in the investment markets, in the case of the IRAs and 401(k)s. After you finish reading what my colleagues and I have assembled here, you will discover that Ms. Novack is advocating a plan that will ultimately force many people to pay more for health care in retirement. Oh, yeah, they'll keep less of their Social Security, too.

Two more advice givers, Dave Ramsey and Suze Orman, try to be more balanced on their Web sites when you request information on annuities. Dave Ramsey seems to be slightly in favor of variable annuities once all other goals are taken care of (namely, your debt is paid off and emergency savings are in place). In my opinion, Dave Ramsey is the expert on getting out of debt. I am encouraged that he sees some good with variable annuities, but he shuns fixed annuities and fixed index annuities for some reason.[90]

Suze Orman openly states that her least favorite annuity is the immediate income type, which is the type that functions like a synthetic pension over a set period of time. In technical annuity terms, we would

89 http://www.forbes.com/sites/janetnovack/2013/08/13/why-dont-retirees-buy-annuities-they-get-something-most-economists-dont/

90 http://www.daveramsey.com/articles/article/articleid/daves-investing-philosophy/category/lifeandmoney_investing/

call this annuitization. She is arguably very open minded about most annuities.[91] But Ms. Orman is confusing creating an income stream with an investment. An investment is something we want to grow. We don't invest to lose. But sometimes things don't pan out our way. Making an investment is like a random walk, which is part of a title of Burton Malkiel's groundbreaking investment and research book, *A Random Walk Down Wall Street*. Or, as my colleague Dan McGrath likes to point out, investing is about a wish and hope. You hope you investment grows. You hope it's there when you need it. You hope you can draw an income off of it. Using an immediate income annuity correctly to complement your investments allows you a little more leeway with trying to achieve your investment goals. Plus, it may have some practical uses when planning for health care in retirement, such as how Medicare treats it.

Allow me to jump on the soapbox for a moment. Please note that any investment vehicle, income strategy, or asset in the wrong situation can be a problem. If you cannot stand to see $1 become $0.96, then don't buy stocks that fluctuate. If you need income, don't invest in vehicles that do not produce income. If you need your money to stay ahead of inflation, why are you using low-yielding investments that cannot keep up with inflation?

I realize I'm being repetitive, but annuities are not about the investment. Sure, there are some new low cost ones that are essentially tax-deferred asset management vehicles. There are often zero guarantees or benefits with these contracts, other than that it is tax deferred and you have multiple investment options. If the investments perform well, you may see some wonderful growth net of fees. But most annuities are about income—how you want to guarantee that income being there— regardless of where interest rates are or how well the stock market is doing. Purer investments, such as individuals stocks and exchange-traded funds (in some case even mutual funds) may grow significantly higher than annuities. But annuities can do one thing investments cannot do: guarantee an income stream.

---

91 http://apps.suzeorman.com/igsbase/igstemplate.cfm?SRC=MD012&SRCN=aoedetails& GnavID=84&SnavID=29&TnavID&AreasofExpertiseID=107

By now you probably have a good handle on the problems my colleagues and I are presenting solutions for which most financial advisors are not even talking about—Medicare and health care expenses in retirement. Even if you agree with our premise, you may not believe in using an annuity for part of the solution. After all, they are one of the more maligned financial products. They are often fully taxable as ordinary income, and there's no step-up in cost basis for your heirs. Despite their shortcomings and the advice of the naysayers, however, annuities can be a very important item in the financial toolbox when you try to stay ahead of the health care time bomb.

How can various types of annuities help you solve some of the problems with paying the potential higher fees for Medicare and health care? Allow me to share some recent conversations with clients about why an annuity will work for them. Every annuity has its niche, and every client has a particular situation where one annuity may work better than another. And yes, it's possible that an annuity doesn't work at all.

Steve is a young professional who has little debt and is a saver. He is opposed to cash building life insurance because people like Suzie Orman said he could do better in other vehicles[92] and Dave Ramsey says to avoid it.[93] I asked him if he had a Roth 401(k) at work. He did not. I asked him did he realize that by maximizing his contributions to a traditional 401(k), he was inflating an asset that will be fully taxed in retirement, would not be accessible to him along the way, and which will potentially be used against him for Medicare premium purposes? He told me, "I'm 42 years old. I put away the maximum allowed in my 401(k). I get a dollar for dollar match up to 6%. I'm good. I am not thinking about Medicare. That's 23 years away. I have health insurance now."

I then asked him if his 401(k) guaranteed, when it's ready to pay out, the income to him. "What do you mean?" he replied. "It's tied to market, but in 23 years I hope it will go up. Check that. I believe it will go up between now and then. It should."

---

92 http://apps.suzeorman.com/igsbase/igstemplate.cfm?SRC=MD012&SRCN=aoedetails&
GnavID=84&SnavID=23&TnavID=&AreasofExpertiseID=160
93 http://www.daveramsey.com/article/the-truth-about-life-insurance/

Steve went into a short discussion on what the historical performance of the equity markets has been since the 1920s. It kind of reminded me of all the awful training I received in the past, before I had the smarts to do my own homework. Then he continued, "When I need the money, I'll sell some stocks or mutual funds."

I politely interrupted him. "Wait, so you're basing your future income on hope? What if your income need comes at a time when the markets are in panic mode, such as the fall of 2008? What if I told you I can guarantee you what your minimum income will be in 23 years if you set aside a minimum of $5,000 today and add a minimum of $5,000 a year for the next 23 years? You can literally build your own pension plan."

Unless you are of a certain age or know of people who are collecting a pension (or will soon), the concept of being paid later with smaller investments today is a tough concept for people to understand. We live in the yo-yo generation, where you're on your own. What this young professional didn't realize was that the income from the annuity I suggested, assuming it was not held in an IRA or qualified retirement plan, would not be fully taxed. The income would be considered a blend of return of premium (amount you put in) and earnings (interest). He would only have to pay taxes on the earnings. We call this the exclusion ratio.

According to *Investopedia*, the exclusion ratio represents a payback of initial investments rather than capital gains. It occurs when one makes a lump sum premium payment or turns over their existing annuity contract to an insurance company in exchange for a series of payments, either over their lifetime or over a set period of time.[94]

What he also didn't know, whether he cared about it or not, is the part of the annuity income that is considered a return of premium is excluded from the modified adjusted gross income (MAGI) calculation for Medicare means testing.[95] So this young professional could exchange part of his retirement hope for a guarantee, and the future income stream has tax and Medicare means testing benefits. This type of

94 http://www.investopedia.com/terms/e/exclusionratio.asp
95 http://socialsecurity.gov/pubs/EN-05-10536.pdf

annuity is called a longevity annuity, which is in effect a deferred income annuity. They are available today from some very large and highly rated insurance companies.

Wait a minute, Rob, if you advise him to do this, he may dial back on some of his 401(k) contributions. That means he'll lose out on tax breaks today. That's exactly what the young professional came back to me with. "My accountant said I am giving up tax breaks today." Here's what I told Steve.

First, I told him to ask his accountant what his effective federal tax rate is[96]. "You're putting away money through salary deferrals. You own a home and have a mortgage and pay property taxes. You have two small children. It's very likely your effective rate is low." I then asked him, "What's going to happen when your kids are grown, the mortgage is paid, and you're retired? What will help you lower your taxable income if you lose out on all those deductions and credits? What happens to your mortgage interest deduction when your mortgage is paid off? What about your dependent exemptions and possible child tax credits when your kids are out of the home and on their own? Do you really believe you'll be in a lower tax bracket in retirement?"

"Okay, Rob, I hear you," he replied. "But I'm thoroughly confused." I told him he didn't have to be confused. "If there's no Roth 401(k) option at work and you earn too much to contribute to a Roth IRA, don't defer money into your 401(k) that is more than the maximum match. In your case, you'll defer 6% of your own money and your employer will match dollar for dollar up to 6% for a total of 12%." The rest of his money earmarked for retirement can go as follows:

1. the longevity annuity we discussed (tax advantage income later)

2. a backdoor Roth IRA if you earn too much to open a Roth (tax-free income later)

3. cash building life insurance (tax-free withdrawals, if structured correctly)

---

96 http://www.investopedia.com/terms/e/effectivetaxrate.asp

Wait, what is a backdoor Roth? It's when you open a nondeductible traditional IRA and then immediately convert it to a Roth IRA.

Speaking of accountants, yours may urge you not to purchase an annuity. It may be because he doesn't understand the product, or it could be purely what he's looking at from a tax standpoint. Distributions from annuities not inside a qualified retirement plan are taxed as ordinary income on the last in first out rules (LIFO). That means you will pay ordinary income taxes on the earnings until you reach your cost basis.[97] You will not receive the benefits of lower tax treatment on stocks, such as qualified dividends and long-term capital gains, or tax-free income like municipal bonds.

The other types of clients suitable for annuities are typically older, the 50 to 60 year olds, but who still have some time on their side. They may want to consider deferred annuities that will allow their future guaranteed income to grow even if the underlying investment subaccounts don't perform. Maybe they need to catch up because the investment markets have been not so favorable (as a whole) over the last 10 to 15 years.

They may not benefit as much from a longevity annuity, unless they want to wait until their 70s or 80s. But what other annuities can potentially do for them may also be worth a look. These annuities are the ones where the investment may grow, lose money, or stay flat, with one twist. It all depends if they are investing in securities or in the movement of indices from one point to another. The future income, not the amount you can surrender the annuity for if you want to cash out, can grow in value. That means your income can be based off of a much higher value than what the underlying cash value may be. Plus, there is one great feature about a nonqualified deferred annuity: You determine when to take the income. Not the IRS with their 70 ½ rules for required minimum distributions, although most companies will force you to annuitize by age 100.

The above factors now become very important when I meet with those in their late 50s and early 60s. The annuity now gives them some control of when to take out income. Yes, almost all of those income ben-

97 http://www.investopedia.com/articles/retirement/05/071105.asp

efits are going to be under the LIFO rules., and yes, your premiums for Medicare Parts B and D at age 65 are going to be based on you modified adjusted gross income at age 63. Then each year after 65 will have a two-year look back period. So why do it? Control. Take out what you can so you don't make Medicare more expensive, and let the accounts that don't increase your Medicare premiums grow so you can use them later. Or take no money out at all.

Now comes an opposite strategy than what the financial services industry has drilled into our minds for years: start withdrawing money out of qualified plans at 59 ½ and pay the tax now (assuming you have the funds to do so). Or, convert the qualified plans to Roth IRAs in the same time frame, but before age 65, again assuming you have the money to pay the extra income taxes. Or maybe you want to move the money to a taxable account where you can control capital gains and the income generated is modest. Lastly, slowly withdraw and buy something that can benefit you later; for instance, an annuity with a long-term care benefit or a life insurance plan with a rider to handle long-term care needs.

Regardless of which option you select, the goal is to shrink the account that will potentially increase your taxable income later. Remember, the deferred accounts mean potentially more taxes and higher expenses for Medicare premiums down the road. You can exercise some control over how to address this, as opposed to the alternative—keep deferring and inflating an asset that won't be all yours.

Ironically, back in the early 2000s, my father went in for a pension consultation that was arranged by his union. He taught junior high school and high school biology in New York City public schools for 31-plus years. He wound up having enough years in before he hit 59 ½ to receive the pension. The advisor told my dad to withdraw at least 1/16 of his 403(b) balance each year starting when he turned 59 ½. When my dad told me this, I thought that was terrible advice. When I retold this story to guys at my Wall Street brokerage firm, they ridiculed the advisor and thought my father should seek another opinion. What moron would want to take early withdraws from a tax-deferred account?

Given what I know now, that was excellent advice. My morons, I mean my parents, did just that. As I type this, they are 67 and they have been slowly reducing their 403(b) balances and paying taxes along the way. Although the advisor my dad met with never mentioned Medicare, he was looking at it from a tax angle and for better protection for the beneficiaries. The advisor was warning my dad that eventually he would have to pay the piper, and it's a much more palatable proposition when you control what the piper will get paid. Also, some 403(b) and other retirement plans have restrictive rules for no spousal beneficiaries. Your kids could be forced to take out the money in either a lump sum or over five years, which could cause them to face a huge tax hit. So that money you deferred for yourself, or as a legacy for your kids if you didn't live long enough to use it, may be chewed apart by the taxman without proper planning.

So if you can afford the taxes on converting your IRA, 403(b), 401(k), etc., to a Roth IRA, and you are under age 63, by all means do it. You'll be grateful in the years ahead.

Additionally, opportunities exist, if you are an accredited investor, which *Investopedia* defines as an individual who qualifies for at least one of the following criteria:

1. Earn an individual income of more than $200,000 per year, or a joint income of $300,000, in each of the last two years and expect to reasonably maintain the same level of income.

2. Have a net worth exceeding $1 million, either individually or jointly with his or her spouse.

3. Be a general partner, executive officer, director, or a related combination thereof for the issuer of a security being offered.[98]

Why is this important? Without launching into a doctoral dissertation, there are some investments that generate up to a 90% loss in the first year, which, depending upon your tax situation, may offset the income generated on the Roth conversion. Certain legal trust work pre-

---

98 http://www.investopedia.com/terms/a/accreditedinvestor.asp

pared by a competent trust attorney may help you reduce the tax liability that would arise from a Roth conversion.

If you are interested in the above and meet the criteria, you are strongly urged to seek advice from competent tax and legal professionals. A wise CPA told me years ago, "Invest because it is a sound investment, not because it sounds like a good tax deal." Well said, and very accurate.

What would I recommend to my clients who are above age 63? And what about the ones who are already in the RMD phase? The answer is to use the use the history of annuities above to your advantage. That is "annuitizing", which is to create your own pension type income. This strategy arguably works best if you are using after tax money.

From a practical real world use of annuities, the payout phase of an annuity will smooth out the sequence of returns. This means that the annuity owner can receive an income stream that will be paid steadily no matter what the stock markets, bond markets, or interest rates do or do not do. The income is paid whether we have a financial panic, like in 2008, or a roaring bull market, as in the latter part of the 1990s. The income will be paid out to you if we go through multiple hedge fund implosions, dot.com busts, 9/11s, etc.

For example, suppose you had a lump sum of money from the sale of an asset or a bonus. Or maybe you have been rolling over certificates of deposit for years. You may want a pension type stream of income to compliment your Social Security, and you don't want to have the risks of the stock market. Perhaps you want your stocks to grow for a later date, or you want to let your tax-free withdrawal accounts, like Roth IRAs, continue to grow. As long as you fund an income annuity with previously taxed money, not all of the income will be taxable when the income is turned on today or later. How is that possible? As we have explained previously, the IRS views some of the income as a return of investment (the so-called exclusion ratio), and some of it as earnings. So this tax advantaged income stream can now give you more wiggle room to plan for income taxes and Medicare premium expenses. Depending on how much income you are already receiving that is subject to the MAGI means testing for Medicare, this tax advantaged income annuity may allow you to add more income to your monthly budget without hitting the higher Medicare income limits. By taking this approach, you may feel more comfortable investing for growth inside Roth IRAs and continuing to defer your cash building life insurance. If you follow the guidelines with Roth IRAs and cash building life insurance, you will be deferring money that may be accessed later—tax-free and free from Medicare means testing.

The exclusion ratio normally applies to immediate income annuities and longevity annuities. The reason is that the income payout is almost always going to be through annuitization. There is, however, one exception I am aware of from the variable annuity market place. One particular company has an IRS ruling and has patented their strategy. The income benefit meets the IRS definition of annuitization without forcing you to completely turn over the contract for a set period of payments. This particular variable contract is a compelling story for those who want the potential appreciation from equity exposure (stock market exposure via mutual funds) plus the additional flexibility of having an income stream that is not fully taxable and not fully means tested for Medicare. Where else can you get the potentially huge benefit of stock market exposure with a vehicle where the income is not fully taxable, and partially free from Medicare means testing? So let that sink in the next time you read something negative about variable annuities!

By now you should have a strong understanding of why an annuity could work for you if you are in your 40s (even 30s) and are thinking about building your own private pension. The same thinking applies if you are in your 50s or early 60s, and want to supplement what you already have done for retirement, or catch up because you are behind schedule. An annuity could work for you if you are already above age 63 and are looking for an attractive income option as well. Remember, an annuity is not technically an"investment,"even though many somewhat ignorant pundits and financial journalists do try to compare them to actual investments. An annuity is an income stream vehicle- it's all about the income—now, in the near future, or many years away.

But what about putting an annuity in a tax sheltered plan, like an IRA?

The kneejerk response is typically "Well, if you do that your adviser is an idiot or is just trying to make a commission. It's inappropriate." An annuity is a tax shelter and so is an IRA. Why on Earth would you want to put a shelter in a shelter? The pundits and annuity haters have been saying this for years. Well, an annuity inside a qualified plan may actually be a great option—if it's set up correctly.

How so? Your required minimum distributions are based on the annuity's contract value, not the potentially higher income withdrawal bucket value. So a bad investment year may require you to take out less, but the amount available for future income may still go up. In other words, you can keep the difference, despite the RMD requirements. What does that mean? It means your required distribution might be 3.5% while your annuity may have a feature, for example, where they will credit up to 6% to the withdrawal base for the first 12 years. But because you took out a 3.5% required distribution, 2.5% will still be credited to your withdrawal account for you to use later. So your annuity, even though it's fully taxable as income because it's in an IRA, may be a lifesaver for you in terms of extra income in retirement (accurate as of the summer of 2013).

The scenario described above is a common one that I run across when I meet people who didn't save enough for retirement, or for those who are underinsured because someone told them they didn't need to have permanent life insurance as part of their plan. If there's no cash value to access from a life policy, then the extra income that the annuity will pay out may prevent investors from raiding other accounts, because they don't have enough money to meet their budget needs. Those other accounts may have more favorable tax treatment and/or may receive more favorable treatment when left for heirs.

How about this situation? If you are over 70 and a half, and your IRA drops significantly in value by December 31, you will be required to take out less the following year to satisfy your required minimum distribution. Great news from a tax standpoint, but what if you wanted to take out more? If you're in a traditionally-funded IRA (holding mutual funds or stocks or bonds or money markets), you're eating into principal to take out this extra money you want or need this year. If you're holding a certain type of annuity in that IRA however, you'll still eat into some principal, but your guaranteed withdrawal provision may let you take out that higher amount and still preserve your base (and possibly more) for future years—even though you lost money! So this type of contract can drop almost to zero, but your income may continue because your income base value was much higher! Are these bad options to have?

Should you pass on an annuity like this in your IRAs? Only you and a competent advisor can make the determination, not those who do not understand the benefits of these guarantees.

Another intriguing example: What if you transfer or rollover money from your other retirement accounts into a qualified annuity (IRA)? What if the performance is awful?. The index crediting option you selected didn't work. The mutual funds in the variable annuity bombed. You're upset at your adviser because you are now underwater and you cannot take a capital loss on if you sell it. Then your advisor points out the following: You have held this variable annuity long enough so that your income base is 200% more than your original investment, even though your original investment is now worth 50% less. What if you did something creative, and completely legal? What if you convert this from an IRA funded with an annuity to a Roth IRA funded with the same annuity contract? The amount of the conversion that is taxable is based on the actual contract cash value, not the higher future income withdrawal base.

Even though you have a loss of money in the contract and taxes will be due on the conversion, the income stream you can turn on will now be tax-free based and an amount greater than what the income would have been on your original investment.

Ask yourself, was this a stupid decision to put an annuity in an IRA that you want to convert later into a Roth IRA? Are annuities so evil inside IRAs?

What if you accumulated a lot but your spouse didn't? How would you like to have the income paid out under a joint life schedule? Some are familiar with this concept for nonqualified annuities. But did you know that it is possible with qualified money, too? Supposed at age 70 you buy an annuity with a withdrawal benefit inside your IRA. You take out minimum distributions to comply with the IRS rules. The account goes up and down. But the future withdrawal amount available keeps rising because you bought an annuity that lets you credit the difference between 6% and your RMD during the first 12 years (available as of 2013). You pass away in the 6th year. Now your spouse has a couple of options.

She could continue the income you were receiving. Or she can exercise the death benefit and take what is left of the original investment after whatever income was taken out. If she cashes it out it, is 100% taxable. But as a spouse, she can roll it into her own IRA and avoid the tax hit at this time. Her decisions are going to be based on whether she needs the higher income or has other assets to replace that income. Lastly, her decisions may be based on what the value of the annuity IRA is at the time of her husband's passing.

These are great options to have. If she was left a lot of life insurance (tax-free death benefit) and other income producing investments to provide enough income, then maybe it's a good idea to exercise the death benefit feature, if the contract is worth a lot less than the withdrawal benefit. She can roll the lower contract value into her IRA. This may be a good strategy to avoid inflating her estate and inflating her RMDs while she is alive. It may allow her to stay under the Medicare threshold for premium penalties. Remember, singles, whether it's by choice or death, you only have half the income threshold for Medicare premiums that a married couple has.

Still think annuities inside a qualified plan are bad? I'll let those for and against annuities spend their time batting that around. They can waste their breath and paper and ink on it. I consider them a flexible wealth management tool. I'd rather look at using annuities to help create a pension for those who don't have a pension. A properly structured annuity plan added to one's other investments can be extremely beneficial for health care and Medicare planning. You get a lot of control and options while you are alive. Structured correctly, they can complement part of your IRA strategy.

My colleagues and I hope that you realize why many people, perhaps yourself included, may need to include an annuity as part of their overall plan. This chapter showed some specific applications and strategies-reasons why you should strongly consider an annuity as part of your financial plan. If you are in the approximately 80% of the population that doesn't have a pension, why not create your own? What is so awful about controlling your cash flow, taxation, and Medicare means testing with an annuity? What is so awful about having an individual investment create income that can last over two (or more) lifetimes? What is so bad about having options to benefit from a Roth IRA conversion?

Summary

- Annuities, when structured correctly in nonretirement accounts, may offer an investor control over when they pay taxes on that income. They do not have to follow required minimum distribution rules (RMDs). This could keep their modified adjusted gross income down (MAGI). They decide when to pay the taxes.

- Annuities, can be used to complement a traditional qualified plan like a 401(k), 457, 403(b), SEP-IRA, SIMPLE-IRA, and may be used to properly unwind your retirement accounts. The first distributions should come out of the plans listed above (contrary to decades of conventional wisdom from Wall Street and financial experts). Annuities with income benefits that may increase if you can wait, may offset some inflation and fill in the gap as you deplete the accounts above. This gives you more time to build up the more favorable tax-free withdrawal accounts (Roth IRAs and loans from cash building life insurance) and more time to do smart tax planning with taxable accounts that allow you to manage gains and losses (e.g., your brokerage account).

- Certain annuities held in nonretirement accounts have a powerful income feature. Part of the income is considered return of investment and part is earnings. The part that is considered return of principal is not taxed as income, and, therefore, does not raise one's MAGI for Medicare premium means testing. These contracts can provide you with this tax advantaged income as long as you live.

- Annuities do have several uses in retirement plans, such as IRAs. For traditional IRAs, they may offer joint income over two lives. This gives the surviving spouse flexibility to continue income or exercise the death benefit payout and comingle the proceeds with his or her owner. This offers some flexibility if there is a concern about MAGI.

- Longevity annuities in non-IRA accounts give the uninsurable (for life insurance) or those without pensions some hope. Instead of facing the typical risks that your investments may underperform, these longevity annuities can give you a worst-case scenario of exactly what your future income will be. In effect, you can plan for a tax-efficient pension. You can also use them to ladder money for future needs, such as how to replace income that may be have been spent down earlier than you had planned.

- Annuities with guaranteed crediting for an income rider might be a great place to park traditional IRA money that may be converted later to a Roth IRA. If the performance is anemic, the guaranteed income still rises. When you convert to a Roth, taxes are due on the accumulation amount and not on the much higher withdrawal base. This may give you additional flexibility if you want to convert, but don't want to do it now. The conversion will preserve that higher income benefit, which will be tax-free from the Roth when turned on.

- Those already holding Roth IRAs may consider using an annuity with an income rider for some of their Roth IRA allocation. In effect, you are creating a tax-free pension for later years. Your account value may drop or stay flat, but many companies offer enhanced income crediting if you can be patient This means you'll receive more tax-free income when you eventually turn on the benefit by exercising the income rider.

12

What's The Deal with Long-Term Care?

By Mike Padawer

(This is an excerpt from Mike's book,
"What's the Deal with Long-Term Care")

What Are The Greatest Myths About Long-Term Care?

While there are many ways to break down the demographics, perhaps it's best to realize that every demographic group has unfortunately bought into the myths regarding Long-Term Care. The most common one is that most people can "self-insure" for their future Long-Term Care expenses.

Unfortunately, those who take this route are hoping to rely on some type of government program to help along the way. Yet, with continued gridlock and partisan bickering in Washington D.C., should anyone *really* expect to depend on politicians to address their future Long-Term Care needs?

The 2012 election opened debate about the future of our country, and a variety of important issues were raised such as Social Security, Medicare and Medicaid –traditionally the "Third Rail" of politics. It's easy to see why these programs are the "800 lb. gorilla" in the room when you consider their ongoing and future costs, along with an official federal debt that now tops $17 trillion.[99] It seems safe to say that one way or another, there are probably some more changes on the way.

Regardless of your political bent, it's impossible to believe that our country can maintain our spending trajectory for Medicare, Medicaid and Social Security along its current path. I'm not going to argue the merits of the solutions presented by either party, but when it comes to dealing with future Long-Term Care expenses, the unfortunate reality is that there are already gaping holes in that safety net.

There seems to be little that the government can do to fix the current problems, as neither party has even presented a proposal to address them in the future. This means it is now time for you and/or your family, to gain a better understanding of Medicare, Medicaid and Social Security, with respect to Long-Term Care concerns, which you are more than likely to encounter in your/their future.

It's important to recognize that Medicare has very limited provisions with respect to covering Long-Term Care expenses. The truth is that relying on Medicare really isn't a viable "solution" and the Medicare website is the easiest place to verify that fact.[100]

If you need another reference point, consider the Social Security statement you used to receive each year. The government stopped sending those statements simply because of the high cost of doing so, but I would encourage you to set up an account with the Social Security Administration under the "my Social Security" section at ssa.gov so you can view your current benefit projections.[101]

Once you register, view your statement and skip to page four, where you will read that ***Medicare does not pay for long-term care, so you may want to consider options for private insurance.***" Whether or not the government makes ANY further changes to the current programs, both Medicare and the Social Security Administration make the point regarding LONG-TERM CARE planning crystal clear!

99 US Debt Clock, http://www.usdebtclock.org/
100 Medicare.gov, "*What's not covered by Part A & Part B?*", http://www.medicare.gov/what-medicare-covers/not-covered/item-and-services-not-covered-by-part-a-and-b.html
101 Official Social Security Website, http://www.ssa.gov/myaccount/

OK, so if Medicare isn't going to help you, what about Medicaid as an alternative?

First, you should understand that Medicaid is considered to be part of the "welfare system"[102] and it has its own limitations on what Long-Term Care is covered, where it's covered and how it's covered. The Medicaid program *today* will cover Long-Term Care needs, but only after you've exhausted nearly all of your assets. Recognize that the key part of the last sentence is the word "*today*"!! With the political and deficit situations we face today, I wouldn't count on Medicaid to cover your Long-Term Care needs **in the future.**

Ignoring the fact that planning on Medicaid as the means for covering your future Long-Term Care needs may be a pipe dream, consider the economic reality of senior care for a moment, and the declining availability of a "Medicaid bed". If you feel that Medicaid could be part of your future, three realities should be considered—(1) You're giving up much of the control of your care, (2)you have limited control over where you receive that care and (3) you intend on becoming destitute (you will no longer have any assets).

Without a Long-Term Care plan of your own, you are essentially "self-insuring" all of your risk of paying for care. Whether people overestimate their ability to pay for care over an extended period, or convince themselves that they'll never need it, the risk of needing and paying for care still remains.

Regardless of your income, or level of assets, having a Long-Term Care plan in place to address the risks and costs of one of the biggest financial threats you may ever face, is a smart move, and can protect both assets and those you love.

What Is The Economic Reality of Long-Term Care?

When you woke up this morning, 10,000 Baby Boomers just turned 65, and this will continue to occur every day for about the next 17 years.[103]

---

102 http://www.thepeoplesview.net/2012/08/medicare-is-welfare-and-so-is-social.html
103 Pew Research Center, "*Baby Boomers Retire*", December 29, 2010

As previously mentioned, roughly 70% of couples aged 65 will experience the need for Long-Term Care at some point in their lives.[104] The degree and duration for which they'll need care remains in question, however, the sheer size of this group will significantly impact the delivery of Long-Term Care services, and the economics of the health care industry as a whole.

According to Ken Dychtwald, president and CEO of the consulting firm Age Wave, *"anyone who thinks the boomers will turn 65 and be the same as the generation before are missing out on the last 60 years of sociology. The boomers change every stage of life through which they migrate. We weren't prepared for the boomers. There weren't enough hospitals or pediatricians. There weren't enough bedrooms in our homes. There weren't enough schoolteachers or textbooks or playgrounds. The huge size of this generation has strained institutions every step of the way."*[105]

It's clear that boomers will have a significant impact on the health care system, especially once it's understood how and where their care will likely be provided. While it may be difficult to simplify this complex topic, we'll attempt to do so by looking at three aspects of the health care system: *Physicians, Home Health Care and Facility-Based Care.*

Doctors Understand Economics 101

In the not-so-distant future, demand for health care (and Long-Term Care services) may very well outstrip available supply, regardless of who provides care or where it's provided. No matter how Washington D.C. tweaks Medicare and Medicaid, or implements the Patient Protection and Affordable Care Act (Obamacare), health care providers won't necessarily choose to participate *if the economics of doing so don't make sense.*

Unfortunately, there seems to be no easy way that our politicians can, or will, effectively address issues with Medicare and Medicaid. Even if changes are made, government cannot simply legislate its way around

---

104 U.S. Department of Health and Human Services website, http://longtermcare.gov/the-basics/who-needs-care/
105 Laura Rowley, The Huffington Post, *"Baby Boomers will transform aging in America, panel says"*, April 2, 2012

the laws of supply and demand. They cannot avoid the economic reality that *supply-side issues* will then dictate price and/or availability. With respect to Medicare and Medicaid, many health care providers will embrace basic economic reality: *They have the ability to "opt out" of providing care under the reimbursement terms of government programs.* It's beginning to happen already.

A recent *Business Week* article highlights the trend of health care providers creating "concierge" practices. *"There aren't enough primary-care people around now,"* says Arthur Caplan, director of medical ethics at the NYU Langone Medical Center. *"When concierge practices spread, that means more and more people will be left without any access to primary care."* Furthermore, by 2020, the Association of American Medical Colleges estimates, there will be 45,000 fewer primary-care doctors than the U.S. needs. *"For the last 13 years, very few students have been going into it,"* says Patrick Dowling, chairman of the department of family medicine at the University of California-Los Angeles's David Geffen School of Medicine. [106]

Based on supply and demand, Americans may be forced to re-evaluate their expectations as to how health care is delivered. If the delivery of health care—*through primary-care physicians*—evolves as Business Week details,[107] the landscape may change throughout the health care system. This could, and likely will, have a direct effect on the delivery and availability of Long-Term Care services as well.

Home Health Care—Maintaining Independence & Choice

Americans love having choices, such as where we live, what we eat, how we entertain ourselves, etc. We are also very selective with respect to our health care. Even if you dismiss the possibility of shortages of physicians in the future, or the potential for a two-tiered delivery system of health care, it's impossible to ignore the fact that every American has a desire to age gracefully and independently—*and in their own familiar surroundings.*

106 Devin Leonard, Bloomberg Business week, *"Is Concierge Medicine the Future of Health Care?"* November 29, 2012
107 ibid

This means the preference for home and/or community based care will continue to become more prevalent as the Boomers continue to age. As such, there will be a substantial increase in the demand for those providing care in this manner. Once again, increasing demand will likely impact the cost and/or the availability of care.

According to the University of California, Center for California Health Workforce Studies, *"there are shortages in the nation's health workforce, particularly among nurses, nursing assistants, home care aides, and personal care workers"* and *"it is important to understand the relationship between the demand for services, the settings in which services will be delivered, and the workforce needed to provide those services."* [108]

In a much more direct way, Shawn Rimerman, owner of ComForcare Senior Services in St. Louis, MO illustrates the problem we face. According to Shawn, *"we go to great lengths to screen our caregivers and finding the right people to work for us, who 1) can care for our clients in the way we expect; and 2) who will do so under today's economic model, is a huge challenge. The demand and the marketplace dictate what we can charge for those services, and simply put, our biggest cost is paying our caregivers a fair hourly rate. As the aging of our population continues, the onus will fall on individuals and families to meet their needs for Long-Term Care services. Realistically, the financial burden of doing so without having to deplete one's life savings cannot be met through any current or potential government program."*[109]

Facility-Based Care: The Good, The Bad & The Ugly

Most people who need medical attention or Long-Term Care services try to avoid facility-based care. Unfortunately, my experience has shown me that because of certain "flaws" with Medicare and Medicaid reimbursement, the reality is that neither program allows for much flexibility, and therefore, facility-based care becomes the norm. This is typically NOT what the patient wants, and it's very expensive for the system overall.

108 University of California, San Francisco, Center for California Health Workforce Studies, *"An Aging U.S. Population and the Health Care Workforce: Factors Affecting the Need for Geriatric Care Workers"*, February 2006

109 INERTIA / Advisor Services Group, *"Long-Term Care: The Economic Reality"*, June 19, 2013

For example, I recently met with a consumer who described a situation where her husband was recovering from a recent surgery, and infections developed during his recovery. Her husband was forced to move to a Long-Term Care facility, where he spent 30 days receiving drug therapy to fight the infections. The only service provided by the facility was a daily visit by a nurse to re-fill the intravenous solution containing the medication. In this instance, Medicare could have saved more than $6,000 had the treatment been allowed in their home, and administered by a private-duty nurse. *And this is happening all around the country*!!

Today, government programs enforce outdated restrictions defining what care can and cannot be provided outside of a medical facility. The lack of cost containment dramatically affects the cumulative cost of health care through these programs overall.. Tomorrow, another 10,000 Boomers turn 65 and this problem will continue to grow!

The Kaiser Family Foundation, a non-profit foundation focusing on the major health care issues facing the U.S, compiles a variety of statistics annually. When you analyze some of the figures, they highlight a somewhat nightmarish scenario. Consider the following statistics:

- There are total of 15,622 Nursing Facilities in the United States.

- The total beds in those facilities equal 1,663,445.

- The occupancy rate for those facilities is currently 83.3%.

- The primary payer for 63% of the residents is currently Medicaid.

- Of the 15,622 facilities, 68% operated on a "for-profit" basis.

- Based on current occupancy, this leaves 300,000 beds "available".[110]

Taken alone, these statistics paint a grim picture. Now combine them with the government's Medicare estimates that by 2020 there will be roughly 20 million people accessing some form of Long-Term Care services.[111]

110 State Health Facts, The Kaiser Family Foundation, *"Certified Nursing Facility Beds"*, http://kff.org/other/state-indicator/number-of-nursing-facility-beds/
111 Centers for Medicare & Medicaid Services, Office of the Actuary, National Health Statistics Group, https://www.cms.gov/Research-Statistics-Data-and-Systems/Statistics-Trends-and-Reports/NationalHealthExpendData/downloads/proj2010.pdf

Maybe Morningstar's recent "40 Must Know Statistics About Long Term Care "estimates are wrong[112] and 40% of those over age 65 WON'T require Facility-Based care at some point in their life, and 10% of those individuals WON'T require care for 5 year or more. If Morningstar's estimates are even partially accurate, simple math tells you by 2020 the country will be in need of approximately 500,000 additional beds. At that point, it won't matter what government programs cover if the 68% of "for-profit" facilities simply choose not participate! *That's the Economic Reality of Long-Term Care!*

Dan McGrath, Director of Institutional Marketing at Zenith Marketing Group sums up the situation, saying Long-Term Care Planning *"is no longer about protecting assets in retirement; it has become the best negotiating chip one can have to access care in retirement".* [113]

Now that you've read this book to this point, hopefully, you take a pragmatic view of the future delivery of health care and Long-Term Care services. I encourage you to embrace the fact that the basic law of supply and demand will likely have far greater impact on the cost, choice and availability of health care, than most people realize today.

---

112 Christine Benz, Morningstar, *"40 Must-Know Statistics About Long-Term Care"*, August 9, 2012
113 INERTIA / Advisor Services Group, *"Long-Term Care: The Economic Reality"*, June 19, 2013

13

The Changing Landscape of Estate Planning
by Justin Belair

Hundreds of years ago, people were unable to designate who would inherit their property upon death, as there was no law that granted them the right to make a will. Circumstances have changed, and now most governments let you keep some of what you have accumulated throughout your lifetime and direct where it goes upon your death. In the United States, your transfer of property is subject to federal estate and gift tax, and many states have either an estate or inheritance tax.

What is estate planning?

Estate planning includes planning for the accumulation, preservation, and disposition of assets during one's lifetime or upon death, as well as nominating a guardian to care for your minor children. Most people, however, equate estate planning simply with the disposition of assets upon death and are familiar with only one vehicle to further such need: the will. Although the will is an integral part of most properly constructed estate plans, it is only one piece.

What is involved in estate planning?

Despite being familiar with wills, it is no secret that over half of all Americans die without one. To avoid having to address the sensitive subject matter, those without one often quip something to the effect of, "I'll be dead, so why should I care?" This statement discounts the fact that estate planning considers lifetime accumulation, preservation, and disposition of one's assets. To account for the fact that so many people die without a will, each state has put in place intestacy statutes to address the issue. Every state has an estate plan for its residents. It may not be the ideal estate plan envisioned by each individual, but it satisfies a pressing need. If the state intestacy laws are unpalatable, then one only needs to create his or her own individual plan that, within broad limits, can be very creative. In fact, a number of states allow you to leave assets in trust for pets, disinherit children, and provide for charitable bequests. Public policy, however, limits the extent to which you may shortchange a spouse, if such a desire is contemplated.

For parents, the will also serves the vital function of nominating a guardian for their minor children and their children's assets. Often overlooked is the fact that although children do not typically have large estates when in the care of their parents, they are funded upon the parents' passing. Most parents would prefer to have a say in who cares for their children if they are not around, yet those preferences go unheard without a will. Consider the thought that goes into determining who will watch the children during a temporary absence, whether it's childcare during working hours, a date night, or a well-deserved vacation. Yet, the same thoughtfulness is ignored for potential permanent absences. Younger people often cite their age as the reason they do not have a will. Actuarially speaking, younger people do have less probability of dying, but not everybody dies of old age. Insurance would be nonexistent if unplanned deaths never happened.

Besides wills, trusts have also become essential estate planning devices. Trusts are legal documents by which a grantor (the trust's creator) transfers legal title to assets to a trustee for the benefit of beneficiaries. They typically come in two forms, revocable and irrevocable. A revocable trust may be changed, amended, or revoked at any time by the grantor. However, such is not the case when dealing with an irrevocable trust. All revocable trusts become irrevocable upon the death of the grantor. In a standard single person revocable trust, the grantor not only establishes the trust, but also serves as the trustee and is the lifetime beneficiary. Family trusts are typically established by both parents for their benefit during lifetime and name the children as successor beneficiaries.

Unlike wills, revocable trusts avoid the need for probate. Probate is the procedure by which the court oversees the administration of one's estate. The probate court appoints an executor, most commonly the one nominated in the will, to be responsible for gathering the decedent's assets, making an inventory of the assets, providing notice to potential claimants and heirs, paying any outstanding debts and taxes, and then distributing the remaining assets in the estate in accordance with the terms of the will. The probate process can be extremely costly and time-consuming. Whereas wills are probated and made a part of the public record, trusts are not. They are private documents that generally do not require judicial oversight. The grantor's wishes are carried out by the successor trustee through private agreement in accordance with the terms of the trust.

Utilizing a revocable trust during one's lifetime does not mean that assets are transferred away or that the grantor loses any control over assets. Since the grantor retains the ability to amend or revoke the trust, the grantor may, therefore, freely remove all or any assets from the trust at any time. In addition, the grantor's Social Security number will be used as the trust's taxpayer identification number and any income or interest earned on the trust's assets will be reported on the grantor's income tax return. However, because the grantor retains complete access to the trust, it will not insulate the assets from the grantor's creditors, nor will it protect trust assets in the event of lawsuits or long-term nursing home care during the grantor's lifetime. With the inclusion of special provisions in the trust, however, the successor beneficiaries will be protected by spendthrift protections.

Trusts are not only great at avoiding probate, but they can also serve as estate tax savings devices. With proper planning, revocable trusts can ensure that the full amount of the estate tax applicable credit is utilized, therefore minimizing the taxes on the grantor's estate. Since the passage of the American Taxpayer Relief Act of 2012, such planning extends to fewer people as the exemption level currently in effect at the time of this writing is $5.25 million per person. When the dust settles surrounding the implementation of the Patient Protection and Affordable Care Act (ACA), an increased focus should be placed upon the distribution of income taxable assets from one's estate. As some Medicare costs are based on the income level of the recipient and are likely to rise, increased consideration must be taken as to how certain inheritances will affect a beneficiary's Medicare costs.

Powers of attorney are legal documents by which a principal appoints an agent to act on his behalf while alive. They typically come in two forms, financial and health care. A power of attorney for financial matters allows the agent to make financial decisions on behalf of the principal. In order for the agent to be able to act should the principal become incompetent, it must be a "durable" power of attorney. A limited power of attorney may be used to allow a spouse to close on the sale of a house in the absence of the other spouse. A durable power of attorney may be utilized by a son or daughter to pay for medical treatment if a parent were involved in an accident and is unconscious, for example.

Durable powers of attorney for health care, or "health care proxies" allow a principal to appoint an agent to make health care decisions on behalf of the principal should he or she is unable to do so because of incapacity or incompetence. So long as the principal can competently make his or her own decisions regarding health care, there is no agency. However, should the principal be unable to communicate such desires to their caregivers either because her or she is incapacitated, unconscious, or incompetent, then the agent would have the power to do so.

Another estate planning document often utilized is the advanced directive or living will. This document usually serves as a backup to the durable power of attorney for health care and is an expression of desire regarding life-sustaining treatment.

Medicaid planning is a specialized niche of estate planning. Certain rules and regulations govern the transfer of assets below fair market value that could render the applicant ineligible for Medicaid benefits for a period of time. Such planning usually contemplates the divestiture of assets to qualify the individual for Medicaid benefits, oftentimes nursing home care. Medicaid trusts, whereby the principal portion of assets is transferred and the income portion is retained, are sometimes employed. Various state and federal laws limit one's ability to utilize this form of planning. For instance, there is currently a "look-back" period of five years on these types of transfers. In addition, some states are implementing laws that are seriously hampering the ability to transfer assets to qualify for Medicaid benefits.

When should an estate plan be drafted?

The most complete answer to the question above is … it varies. Everyone's situation is different. After meeting with hundreds of clients, however, a pattern has emerged. Clients will usually come in at one of three periods in their lives: they just had a child, their children have matured to the point where they can make competent decisions, or they are either contemplating retirement or have just retired.

New parents want to have a say in who raises their children should an unexpected tragedy occur. A will and durable powers of attorney are necessities. Although an estate plan should be reviewed every five years, at a minimum, estate plans often sit unattended for much longer periods of time. These same parents often return once their children have matured to update their plans. Other parents who neglected to ever put an estate plan in place when they had minor children also may decide to effectuate a plan. Now that the children are old enough to act in the capacity of fiduciaries—agents, executors and trustees—it provides parents with additional options. Moreover, the original named fiduciaries are probably much older and may no longer be around to function in that role. Finally, just prior to or upon retirement, it is common for people to seek guidance regarding an estate plan. The accumulation stage has ended and individuals will now begin living off of the fruits of their labor. At this stage people have a good idea of what their assets are, to whom they should go, and who they want to manage their affairs.

It must also be noted that estate plans should be reviewed upon the occurrence of any major life event such as the death of a spouse or a divorce. An unattended estate plan may cause unnecessary headaches at a later date. In addition, estate planning is not something that should be put off until the last possible minute. Although an effective estate plan can be implemented when one is terminal, it is better to have time as an ally and not as an enemy.

Why is estate planning necessary?

Although each state has its own intestate succession statutes for probate assets, most favor the surviving spouse and children. For example, should one die leaving a spouse and children, a common scheme would see the spouse take a lump sum and then split the balance with the children. However, if the decedent is unmarried and does not have children, then the parents, if living, are usually next in line. A first blush, this seems reasonable. What happens if the decedent is 70 years old and his 95-year-old mother has been on state assistance in a nursing facility? All of the decedent's assets would pass to his mother, her state assistance would end, and her care would consume those assets.

It is becoming more common for couples to cohabitate without formalizing their commitment to one another through marriage. Without advanced planning, upon the death of one partner, the surviving partner is not entitled to any of the assets of the deceased partner. Moreover, should one partner become incapacitated in any manner, a court battle could loom between the healthy partner and immediate family members of the other partner, if there were conflicting views over life-sustaining treatment.

Blended families are also becoming more prevalent. Although adopted children are automatically taken into consideration under most intestate succession laws, stepchildren are not. The only way to ensure stepchildren share in any distribution is to properly plan for it.

Some couples are choosing not to have children. Without children in the equation, once parents are no longer around, consideration must be given to who will benefit from the estate and who will serve as fiduciaries.

People have become more transitory. The "Greatest Generation," by and large, stayed put. After returning from World War II, they settled down and raised family, often establishing deep roots in their community. They typically worked at the same job for long periods of time and most owned a home where they lived for the duration of their lives. Today, people stay put for much shorter periods of time. People move more frequently and split time between states. If a person dies owning assets in multiple states, multiple probates may be necessary. Imagine simultaneously overseeing a probate in New York, Colorado, and Florida. Trusts can help to eliminate this hardship.

Trusts also allow for increased control over assets passed to beneficiaries. Despite parents' best efforts to instill in their children sound financial acumen, their children may not have the same affinity for handling their financial affairs as their parents did. Trusts can provide certain protections against creditors and place limits on how much and when a child receives distributions. The "dead hand" can continue to guide long after a parent is gone.

As mentioned earlier, estate planning also includes planning for the accumulation and preservation of assets. Life insurance can be placed in an irrevocable life insurance trust to remove it from one's gross estate while still ensuring that the intended beneficiary receives the benefit, or that it can be used to preserve the value of illiquid assets in the estate.

An illiquid estate can pose many problems for heirs and beneficiaries. If an estate is comprised primarily of real estate or minority business interests, then liquidity (the ability to easily sell an asset for cash at fair market value) could be an issue. Paying the burial, administration, and taxes are a concern and should be considered as part of any good estate plan. Having to sell the vacation home in Nantucket or the family business because the estate does not have enough cash to cover the costs is not an ideal situation, especially when a little bit of planning could have prevented this outcome.

If charitable endeavors are contemplated, the use of charitable trusts may be an effective way of accomplishing such intentions. Depending on one's financial picture, certain charitable trusts may be crafted in such a way as to divert taxable income from the estate during the life of the grantor while ensuring that the remaining assets are distributed to the grantor's intended beneficiaries.

Conclusion

People have undertaken estate planning for hundreds of years and will continue to for hundreds more. It is not a new concept, yet, with ever changing tax, social, and medical laws, it is imperative that capable counsel be sought. An increased dialogue between lawyers, tax professionals, and financial planners will aid in the advice provided to those who seek assistance.

Young or old, wealthy or poor, every person should undertake some form of estate planning. Whether that estate plan includes wills, revocable trusts, durable powers of attorney, and life insurance trusts, or just joint accounts and beneficiary designations, depends on the person and their circumstances. Estate plans are as unique as the people who utilize them.

14

The Facts About Reverse Mortgages
by John Marroni

The budget should be balanced
The Treasury should be refilled
Public debt should be reduced
the arrogance of officialdom should be tempered and controlled
And the assistance to foreign lands should be curtailed, lest Rome will become bankrupt.
People must again learn to work instead of living on public assistance.
—Cicero, 55 BC

How would you like to remain in your home and never worry about paying your bills including your mortgage, credit cards, utilities, and health care costs?

How would you like to remain in your home, never have to make a mortgage payment, and have money coming in every month without tapping into your investments?

How would you like to downsize to a new home, never make a mortgage payment, and have more cash than you ever dreamed you would have?

A reverse mortgage can help you achieve all of these scenarios, and much more.

A reverse mortgage is a special type of loan that enables homeowners age 62 and over to tap the equity they have in their home and receive tax-free income. Unlike a traditional home equity loan, no repayment is required until the home is no longer the primary residence.

Eligibility

- The homeowner must be at least 62 years old and occupy the property as their primary residence.
- The home must be owned free and clear or have only a small remaining mortgage balance.
- The property can be a single family dwelling up to four units as well as HUD approved condominiums.
- There are no income, asset, employment, or credit requirements on a reverse mortgage.

Tax-Free Options

- Lump sum advances make cash available for immediate use.
- Tenure (monthly payment) plans provide fixed monthly cash advances for life or for a fixed period of time, whichever the borrower chooses.
- A line of credit makes cash available when requested by the borrower, as needed.
- The borrower may select a combination of payments options to suit individual needs.

How Much Can The Borrower Receive?

You can find a great reverse mortgage calculator on the HUD Web site.[114] Once there, type in "reverse mortgage calculator" under "search" and you will be sent to the calculator.

What Are Some of the Benefits of a Reverse Mortgage?

- Tax-free income does not affect Social Security or Medicare benefits.

---

114 www.hud.gov

- Homeowners retain title to the property at all times.

- No repayment is required until the homeowner dies, moves, or sells the home.

- With a nonrecourse loan, no deficiency judgment can be placed against the borrower or their heirs. Neither the borrower nor the heirs will ever be responsible for any amount exceeding the balance of the loan or the sales proceeds of the house, whichever is less (e.g., if the balance of the loan is $400,000 and the house sells for $300,000, neither the borrower nor the heirs are responsible for the $100,000 deficit).

- No credit, asset, or health questions to obtain a reverse mortgage.

- Funds can be used for most any purpose.

- Travel

- Medical bills

- Home improvement

- Payoff existing mortgage

- Delay nursing home stay

- Supplement current income

The following are real-life scenarios as to why people have obtained reverse mortgages:

1. *Paying off your existing mortgage and credit card debt with a reverse mortgage.*

A married couple had been living in the home they bought when they first got married 50 years ago. This was the house their children grew up in. Their grandchildren, whose ages range from 15 to 26, live close by and frequently visit them. This is like a second home to these grandchildren. Over the years, they continually took cash out of their home to pay for various expenses, including their children's college education. They had last refinanced for a mortgage of $400,000 and could no longer afford the $2,000 per month mortgage payment. They also had $30,000 in credit card balances that required them to pay a minimum payment of $600 per month. Their home was worth $800,000. They did not want to sell their home and downsize to a home they could afford, which would mean moving away from their children and grandchildren. They resolved this problem by obtaining a reverse mortgage to pay off their current mortgage as well as pay off all their credit cards. This reverse mortgage enabled them to free up $2,600 per month and allow them to remain in their home. Because of the nature of the reverse mortgage, they were not required to make monthly payments as long as they lived in their home.

2.   *A homeowner takes out a reverse mortgage for Tenure (monthly payment) plans to provide fixed monthly cash for 8 years in lieu of drawing against her retirement fund.*

A 62-year-old widow had been living in her home that was worth $600,000. She had no mortgage on the property and did not want to move. She was contemplating on drawing against her retirement funds, which she would have to claim as income and pay taxes. I had sat with her and her financial planner and showed them that if she obtained a reverse mortgage, she could receive the same amount of money on a monthly basis, tax free, as if she were drawing against the retirement fund. By not touching the retirement fund, this gave her the opportunity to let her money grow considerably for the next 8+ years before she would even have to access the funds while receiving money from the reverse mortgage monthly payments.

3.   *Purchasing a home using a reverse mortgage.*

A married couple, both 67 years old, was living in the home they owned. They were at the point where the home was too big for them and were struggling to make the mortgage payment. In fact, they were three months behind on their mortgage and would soon be receiving letters from the bank to start the foreclosure process. Their home was worth $600,000 and owed $400,000 on the mortgage (not enough equity for a reverse mortgage). Long story short, they were able to sell their home for $600,000 and, after paying the realtor's commission and back taxes, walked away with $150,000 in their pocket. This amount was not enough to buy a home. And because their credit was poor due to the recent mortgage payment history, they were unable to obtain a traditional mortgage. One of the benefits of a reverse mortgage is that it is not based on credit or income. It is based on a person's age. They ended up buying a small ranch for $275,000 and obtaining a reverse mortgage for $150,000, requiring them to put down $125,000. They still had $25,000 left in their bank after the transaction and were not required to make a mortgage payment. This reverse mortgage saved their financial life. They went from almost losing their home and being out on the street to living in a home mortgage and worry free.

These were just a few of the countless scenarios a reverse mortgage can do for you and your family.

If It Is So Good, Why Doesn't Every Qualified Borrower Get a Reverse Mortgage?

There has been a lot of negative press in regards to taking out a reverse mortgage. The following are the most common I hear:

1. The closing costs are too high.

Among the negatives of a reverse mortgage are the costs involved. All mortgages have costs, but reverse mortgage fees, which can include the interest rate, loan origination fee, mortgage insurance fee, appraisal fee, title insurance fees, and various other closing costs, are high when compared with a traditional mortgage; however, these costs have dropped dramatically over the past few years. The good news is the closing costs are not paid out of pocket, but rolled into the loan.

2. The bank can foreclose on the home.

Another potential issue to be aware of is the requirement to pay back the loan if you should permanently move out of the home. This may not sound like a problem now, but if you ever need to enter a full-time care facility, the loan would become due if you left your home for a year or more. Another alternative to selling the home is to have your heirs refinance your reverse mortgage with a traditional mortgage (if it makes sense).

3. The lender takes title to the home and when you sell, the lender keeps the proceeds.

You still retain ownership of your home. The reverse mortgage is only a lien against the property. The proceeds are disbursed just the same if there were a traditional mortgage on the home.

4. Children will lose their inheritance.

A common downside to the reverse mortgage is the fact that it affects your estate. The reverse mortgage will almost always decrease the equity in your home, which will leave less money to your heirs. This one can be a personal issue if it is important that you leave some inheritance to your heirs. If this is the case, you may want to have candid discussions with them in regards to your current financial situation. You may find that your heirs may find it more important that you are financially sound and may not even care nor even expect an inheritance.

5. A reverse mortgage can cause you to be evicted from your home.

You leave your home when you choose. No one will force you from your home. The reverse mortgage is not due until your home is no longer your primary residence. However, you will still be required to stay current on property taxes, keep the home in good repair, and maintain applicable insurance on the home.

6. A reverse mortgage could affect your eligibility for Social Security and Medicare.

Social Security and Medicare will not be affected; however, borrowers with Medicaid or Social Security Supplement may lose eligibility. These programs required a monthly income of less than $2,000, which could have a negative impact by the funds from a reverse mortgage.

7. If the value of the home is less than the outstanding balance of the reverse mortgage, then the homeowner or their heirs will be responsible for the difference when they go to sell the home.

A reverse mortgage is a nonrecourse loan, meaning that the lender cannot legally demand more that the value of the home at the time of closing. This means that the lender will pay any difference between the home value and the loan balance.

When deciding whether a reverse mortgage is right for you, you should consult with your heirs, financial advisor, and tax professional, as well as an elder law attorney. You need to evaluate the pros and cons of obtaining a reverse mortgage. In most cases, you will find that obtaining a reverse mortgage will have a tremendous positive impact to your current financial position. It is a great tool that is not utilized enough.

Whether you are bank rich or bankrupt, self-employed or unemployed, a reverse mortgage can help you increase your net worth and finance your American Dream.

15

Afterword

by Jack Tatar

When Dan McGrath first contacted me about my being involved on a book about retirement, he assured me that it would not be your "typical" retirement book. He promised it would discuss topics that were timely, relevant, and somewhat controversial pertaining to the financial implications of retirement.

I was willing to listen because, like Dan, I, too, was not interested in seeing yet another retirement book that focused on what someone thought was the best way to allocate assets or build an income stream for retirement.

In other words, I didn't want it to be yet another book that treats retirement as nothing more than just a financial situation and can solve all of your problems with a unique portfolio allocation process the author came up with.

In 2011, after losing both my parents, I felt I needed to write a book that focused on what I saw as the real needs of those individuals and couples who are either about to retire or are already retired. I wanted my book to explore what I had learned from my own parents' situation, which is that retirement is not just about having enough money, but rather it's a new stage of life that demands an approach that goes beyond just finances.

After examining the research I had gathered on retirement through my company, GEM Research Solutions,[115] along with my personal experience regarding my own parents' retirement, I wrote my book, *Safe 4 Retirement: The Four Keys to a Safe Retirement*,[116] which examines the need for taking a more holistic view of retirement in order to create a later life in which retirees can thrive and, ultimately, live longer.

My holistic approach to retirement is based on the premise that having a safe and lengthy retirement requires more than just being financially prepared. It requires that retirees and pre-retirees consider what I call the "four keys to a safe retirement," which includes not only financial preparedness but also health and wellness, mental attitude, and the need to stay involved.[117]

When I began to consider the market for my book, I found that most retirement books today dealt primarily with the aspects of having enough money to retire and what to do with it. The shelves at Barnes & Noble and on Amazon are filled with so-called retirement experts telling you whether or not you should buy bonds or stocks and how to allocate them. It further amazed me at how many books could be written on this topic and stay on the shelves for years, even though the rules of retirement had clearly changed.

Aside from the lack of books that consider health, wellness, attitude, and community involvement as keys for any one's later life, there are shelves and shelves of retirement books that still leave out the realities of Social Security, health care costs, and long-term care alongside their "advice" on asset allocation and portfolio management.

When I brought up this point with Dan, he agreed and cited that "when they do include these topics, most times they haven't updated their information or they're just flat out wrong!"

Dan clearly had my attention, and he went with it.

---

115 http://www.GEMResearchSolutions.com
116 http://Safe.PeopleTested.com
117 http://www.marketwatch.com/story/the-four-keys-to-a-safe-retirement-2012-12-13

"What we want to do is create a book that tells people what the realities of today's retirement looks like," Dan said. "The problem is that there is so much that people don't know about retirement, and because of that, people are getting hurt. Lives are being impacted because the plans they worked with for years have been upended by new laws and political decisions."

Dan's approach was to create a book that warned people that what they don't know about retirement could hurt them. He wanted to assemble a group of knowledgeable professionals who had worked in the financial services area for years and have them write on their subject of expertise.

He promised me that the book would be opinionated. Now that you have read it, you have probably seen that to be true.

He also felt that the book would be controversial.

The book that you have just read is not controversial because it discusses the ineffectiveness of Washington and addresses items like Obamacare. It is controversial because of the question that Dan posed early in this book: "If even a seasoned investment professional like myself didn't know things about retirement that could hurt others, how could I truly help anyone to navigate through their retirement?"

I have always been, and still am, a proponent of working with a trusted financial advisor to plan and execute your retirement plan. I also believe that the best financial advisors have begun to undertake a more holistic view of retirement for their clients and have integrated health care and wellness planning and are helping their clients stay active and involved in their communities.

As the new world of retirement changes, financial advisors also need to change how they do business and how they view their clients.[118] This requires they take a holistic approach to retirement. I also believe that it requires them to involve the adult children of their retiring or retired

---

118 http://www.marketwatch.com/story/is-your-financial-advisor-an-endangered-species-2013-08-13

clients in discussions around health care proxies, wills, estates, and tracking information, such as medications and doctors, regarding their parents.[119]

When you add in the realities of including the complexities of Social Security, health care plans, and Medicare in the equation, many advisors are throwing their hands up, recognizing that it's just become "too much" of a challenge to keep up with all of it.

There are certainly many advisors who have thrown their hands up and have kept them up. They fall back into their comfort zone of advising you about stocks and bonds or which money manager you should be investing with.

Will they be the ones that, as Dan asks, can "truly help anyone" with the new realities of retirement that you have just read about in this book?

I remain an eternal optimism and believe that because most advisors who run their own business most honestly care about the well-being of their clients, they will recognize that they need to learn the things about retirement that most of us don't know, just as you have done by reading this book.

We're seeing some of that today as some major firms are requiring their advisors to integrate health care discussions into retirement plans and regular reviews so they can help their clients make the best decisions on these items. We're seeing organizations such as the Retirement Income Industry Association educating their advisor on the complexities of Social Security and building new credentials that require them to include health care options into retirement plans.[120]

Five years ago these were not items that the average financial advisor was considering for their client. The thinking back then was that no advisor gets paid on health care or Social Security, so why should they spend the time advising clients on it? The sad fact is that for many advisors, that's still their thinking today.

---

119 http://www.marketwatch.com/story/having-the-talk-about-retirement-2012-12-24
120 http://riia-usa.org/training/default.asp

So here you are, at the end of a book that Dan promised me would make an impact on people's thinking about retirement and how to plan for it. I'll leave it up to you if Dan fulfilled his promise, but I look back fondly on my decision to be involved with this book.

This is a necessary book.

This is a wake-up call for anyone who thinks they are financially prepared for retirement.

I believe that there are many things that have been explored in this book that justify the title that Dan gave to this book: *What You Don't Know About Retirement Will Hurt You.*

After I finished reading what the other financial services professionals wrote in this book, I found myself contemplating Dan's question from his introduction, "The question is, what are you going to do with this information?"

I invite all of you, now that you have read this book, to discuss this book's contents with not only your friends and families, but also with your financial advisors as well.

How they react to this information may tell you much about them and how they intend to help you in this new world of retirement.

About the Authors

Michael Gerali

Mike, a Colorado native, is a founding partner of HRSolutions & Brokerage, LLC (HRSB). He's co-Founder of Jester Financial Technologies, the leading firm in the nation when it comes to calculating out-of pocket health care costs in retirement. He has been active in the employee benefits and human resources consulting arena since 1989 and served as President of HR Source prior to his founding of HRSB. He specializes in all aspects of employee benefits including, group health insurance, dental, vision, life, short term and long term disability and long term care insurance. Mike obtained his ChFC designation in 1997 and his CLU in 2009. In 2013 Mike passed his CFEd exam and is a registry member of HIFE.

Most recently, he has been a featured speaker at numerous national conferences on the topics of Retiree Pension and Healthcare Obligations. He is a graduate of the University of Colorado at Boulder with a Bachelor of Science degree in Finance. He lives in Denver with his wife Allyson and his two daughters.

Michael's contact information:

Website: www.hrsolve.com
Email: mgerali@hrsolve.com
LinkedIn: www.linkedin.com/pub/michael-gerali-clu-chf-c/14/669/81a/

Dan McGrath

Mr. McGrath has over 20 years of broad financial and healthcare-research experience. He's co-Founder of Jester Financial Technologies, the leading firm in the nation when it comes to calculating out-of pocket health care costs in retirement. Mr. McGrath has authored numerous articles and publications on the topics of Medicare and healthcare in retirement, including the whitepaper "Assessing the Inevitable Cost of Healthcare in Retirement". He lives in Windham, NH with his wife and 4 children.

Dan's contact information:

Email: dmcgrath@jesterfinancial.com
LinkedIn: www.linkedin.com/in/retirementhealthcarecosts/

Justin Belair

Justin S. Belair graduated from Boston College Law School in 2002. He has been licensed as a Massachusetts attorney for over ten years and has worked at the Law Offices of Gould & Gould for the past three years. The Law Offices of Gould & Gould is a general practice law firm with offices located in Londonderry, NH, Hooksett, NH and Andover, MA. Justin specializes in the areas of estate planning, real estate, and business.

Justin's contact information:

Email: justin.belair@gouldnhlaw.com

Rob Klein

Rob Klein is an independent financial advisor who has over 15 years of planning experience who specializes in working with individuals and small business owners to ensure that in their retirement the concerns of income, taxes and health care have been solved. Rob lives in White Plains, NY and is married with two sons, ages 3 and 4.

Rob's contact information:

Email: ardmoregroup@gmail.com
LinkedIn: www.linkedin.com/in/advisorrob

John Marroni, NMLS ID#5778

John Marroni, a long standing veteran of the mortgage and lending field who began working as a mortgage broker in the summer of 1995 and in 2000, he became one of the partners with New Boston Mortgage. John, one of the first innovators and leaders on Reverse Mortgages can be heard as a co host for the radio show 'The Mortgage Forum' heard on WESX and WBNW in Boston MA. John graduated from Northeastern University with a BS in Industrial Engineering in 1988.

John's contact information:

Website www.johnmarroni.net
Email john@johnmarroni.net
LinkedIn www.linkedin.com/in/johnmarroni/

Mike Padawer

Mike Padawer has more than two decades of experience in the financial services arena; including roles in retail, wholesale and sales management functions. Today, he focuses solely on working with advisors and institutions; providing customized Long Term Care planning solutions for their individual, group and business owner clients. Mike's background also includes successful implementation of training, coaching and Continuing Education programs which have helped hundreds of advisors meet the financial planning needs of their clients. Mike resides in Chesterfield, Missouri. He enjoys live music, playing golf and ice hockey, and traveling with his children.

Mike's contact information:

Website www.whatsthedealwithltc.com
Email mike@whatsthedealwithltc.com
LinkedIn www.linkedin.com/pub/mike-padawer/3/449/b4/

Bob Ryerson

Robert M. Ryerson has been a financial advisor since 1984, and a Certified Financial Planner since 1991. Robert is also a Certified Identity Theft Risk Management Specialist, a notary public, and a news junkie who is increasingly concerned about the state of affairs in the headlines he sees these days. He is happily married with four beautiful daughters.

Bob's contact information:

Website: www.newcenturyplanning.com
Email: rryerson@newcenturyplanning.com
LinkedIn: www.linkedin.com/in/robertmryerson/

Jack Tatar

Jack Tatar is known as "America's Safe Retirement Coach" and is the author of three books that are changing how people view retirement. His first, "*Safe 4 Retirement: The Four Keys to a Safe Retirement*" lays out his foundational approach to viewing retirement in a holistic fashion by including the Four Keys: Financial Preparedness, Health & Wellness, Mental Attitude and Staying Involved into planning for retirement. His latest book is "*Having The Talk: The Four Keys to Your Parents' Safe Retirement*", which lays out the need and plan for having that necessary "talk" between retired or retiring parents, and their children and family about later life issues. He writes regularly for Marketwatch.com as one of their RetireMentors.

Jack's contact information:

Website: www.safe4retirement.com
Email: Jack@safe4retirement.com
LinkedIn: www.linkedin.com/in/jacktatar/

www.ingramcontent.com/pod-product-compliance
Lightning Source LLC
LaVergne TN
LVHW021458080426
835509LV00018B/2333